The *Art* of
School
Leadership

Thomas R. Hoerr
Foreword by Roland S. Barth

Association for Supervision and Curriculum Development
Alexandria, Virginia USA

Association for Supervision and Curriculum Development
1703 N. Beauregard St. • Alexandria, VA 22311-1714 USA
Phone: 800-933-2723 or 703-578-9600 • Fax: 703-575-5400
Web site: www.ascd.org • E-mail: member@ascd.org
Author guidelines: www.ascd.org/write

Gene R. Carter, *Executive Director;* Nancy Modrak, *Director of Publishing;*
Julie Houtz, *Director of Book Editing & Production;* Genny Ostertag, *Project Manager;*
Reece Quiñones, *Graphic Designer;* Cynthia Stock, *Typesetter;* Dina Murray Seamon,
Production Specialist

All Web links in this book are correct as of the publication date below but may have
become inactive or otherwise modified since that time. If you notice a deactivated
or changed link, please e-mail books@ascd.org with the words "Link Update" in the
subject line. In your message, please specify the Web link, the book title, and the page
number on which the link appears.

ASCD Member Book, No. FY06-03 (December 2005, P). ASCD Member Books mail
to Premium (P), Comprehensive (C), and Regular (R) members on this schedule:
Jan., PC; Feb., P; Apr., PCR; May, P; July, PC; Aug., P; Sept., PCR; Nov., PC; Dec., P.

Paperback ISBN 1-4166-0229-1 • ASCD product #105037

e-books: retail PDF ISBN 1-4166-0310-7 • netLibrary ISBN 1-4166-0308-5 •
ebrary ISBN 1-4166-0309-3

Quantity discounts for this book: 10–49 copies, 10%; 50+ copies, 15%; for 500 or more
copies, call 800-933-2723, ext. 5634, or 703-575-5634.

Library of Congress Cataloging-in-Publication Data

Hoerr, Thomas R., 1945–
    The art of school leadership / Thomas R. Hoerr ; foreword by Roland S. Barth.
      p. cm.
    Includes bibliographical references and index.
    ISBN 1-4166-0229-1 (alk. paper)
  1. School management and organization. 2. Educational leadership. I. Title.

    LB2805.H585 2005
    371.2'00973—dc22
                                           2005019540

12 11 10 09 08 07 06 05   12 11 10 9 8 7 6 5 4 3 2 1

With much affection and respect, this book
is dedicated to the entire New City School
community. From students to staff members,
from parents to neighbors, from friends to
administrators, from alums to teachers,
I owe so much to everyone here.

The Art of School Leadership

Foreword

Some dream. Some enact the dreams of others. Very few dream and then follow those dreams. Even fewer write about this.

In the pages that follow, you will discover that Tom Hoerr does all four. So sit back. You are about to embark on a field trip to New City School in St. Louis, Missouri, without leaving your comfortable chair!

Craft knowledge is the wisdom that educators necessarily accumulate by virtue of spending 6 or 8 or 10 hours a day, 220 days a year, under the roof of a schoolhouse. Craft knowledge is what we learn about teacher and principal leadership, relationship building, staff development, goal setting, power, and teacher evaluation. It's what we come to know about creating a culture of creativity, building teams, running effective faculty meetings, and increasing parent involvement.

I have long believed that if only teachers and administrators would unlock, celebrate, and disclose their abundant craft knowledge, we could transform our schools overnight. Regrettably, in our profession, very little craft knowledge *is* disclosed. Those teachers who retire next June will leave, taking with them all they have learned in the school of hard knocks over their careers—knowledge and skills that will never again be available to the school. What a tragic loss to the school, to youngsters, to colleagues, and to the educator who never had the opportunity to share.

There are good reasons, of course, why craft knowledge is not shared. The cruel reality is that our profession places us in the role of competitors for scarce recognition and resources. The better you look, the worse I look; the worse you look, the better I look. So we keep our gems hidden away.

Too often, the educator who has the courage to disclose craft knowledge at a faculty meeting ("I've got this great idea I want to share about linking science and literature!") is greeted by glazed eyes or critical glowers. "Who does she think she is?" So we soon learn to keep what we glean from our school experience tightly locked up.

What you are about to read is the revelation of Tom Hoerr's craft knowledge and that of scores of teachers and parents with whom he has worked for some 28 years. You will soon discover here, as I have, helpful, concrete ideas about ways to expand your repertoire in dealing with recurring school issues, from underperforming teachers to leadership to parent involvement.

It's a rare and welcome opportunity to be invited inside the school and the mind of a fellow educator and have that person hand over the "keys to the store." I hope that others will follow and profit from Tom's example.

Alas, here we run up against another enduring impediment so engrained in the culture of our schools. In our profession, we are gifted and talented at finding reasons and excuses why good ideas in one school cannot possibly work in "my" school.

• They have all that Title I money to spend on their program.

• They have more freedom with their curriculum than the central office gives *us*.

• They have all those rich white kids to whom you can teach anything.

• They have parents who will support teachers' efforts.

And so it goes.

Tom Hoerr's New City School is a nonpublic, independent school. A common belief within independent schools is that they *are* independent and therefore can innovate without bureaucratic restraints. Many also believe their new ideas and practices will soon be noticed, valued, and emulated by those in public schools. I certainly never found this to be the case when I worked in either an independent or a public school! So it is very easy to dismiss what follows as irrelevant and impossible to relate to "my" school.

Don't be deceived. For the important issues and opportunities that confront schools are generic. *All* schools deal with underperforming teachers, staff development, teacher empowerment, curriculum, and other recurring elements of school life. What is different is how each school responds to these similar conditions. Sadly, all too often the response is discouragingly uniform: A faculty meeting is a time when the principal stands at the front and proclaims while the teachers sit and listen (maybe!).

That is the gift of this volume. Its author, after nearly three decades, is still dedicated, energized, hopeful—and learning. What he has learned and continues to learn constitutes a compendium of refreshingly *different* ways of thinking about school and about how to lead adults and students in the service of the central purposes of the school. Here, after many turbulent years as a school leader, is one who not only respects teachers, he also likes them! His *is* a "new school" that offers new ways of thinking about promoting profound levels of human learning. These ideas can be replicated in other schools with no change in budget, only a change of heart.

Several conditions are necessary for a successful transfer of craft knowledge. One has to have some craft knowledge to share. One has to be courageous and willing enough to share it. One has to have others who will welcome and value the sharing. And there is a fourth necessary condition: One has to be able to make one's craft knowledge accessible to others through oral and written language. Again, Tom Hoerr succeeds admirably in this regard.

A central theme of this book is that "leadership is about relationships." Tom Hoerr walks the talk. He will succeed with you, I suspect, as he has with me, in establishing a strong, engaged relationship. Through playfulness, joyfulness, honesty, and jargon-free authenticity, he earns credibility and respect. His depiction of life in the schoolhouse will resonate with the experiences of most teachers, administrators, and parents.

Aldous Huxley once observed, "Experience isn't what happens to us, it's what we *make of* our experience." I think you will find here a multitude of school experiences. And you will find that Tom Hoerr has indeed made something of them. I would like one day to visit New City School and linger with this extraordinary educator and his faculty. Fortunately, none of us has to wait. Enjoy the field trip!

Roland S. Barth

Acknowledgments

Writing this book is another step in my professional journey. It has been a fun journey, sometimes frustrating, never boring, and always gratifying. Like most travelers, I have repeatedly been helped along the way by knowledgeable and kind others. Sometimes I knew that I was lost and asked for directions. At other times, I was positive that I knew the way, but, in fact, I was simply walking in circles; walking faster, but still in a circle. Whatever success I have is due to the many, many people who have taken the time to share their thoughts with me, to listen to my ideas, to agree and to disagree, and to cause me to reflect upon and question my ideas. This isn't as easy as it may sound. There is a reason why the saying on my coffee mug reads, "Often wrong, never in doubt."

Where to begin? Thanks go, first, to the faculty of New City School. I am extraordinarily fortunate to work with such a talented, caring, and energetic group of teachers. I am often in awe of the magic that they bring to their classrooms each and every day. They are tolerant of my ideas and puns, good and bad. The Board of Trustees of New City School has been wonderfully supportive, and I appreciate their confidence and wisdom. I never thought that I would work so long in one setting, but I find myself eager to go to work each day, simultaneously supported and challenged. Our students and our parent body, as well as the other staff members, also deserve thanks. New City School truly is an exceptional place, and I am proud of what all of us have accomplished.

Many individuals whose paths I have crossed have left a lasting imprint on me. Various drafts of chapters from this book were read by numerous others, and their feedback was always helpful. Scores of teachers from around the world offered comments that clarified and moved my thinking forward. At the risk of neglecting to mention someone to whom I am indebted (which will invariably happen, I realize), I would like to thank the following for their support and inspiration: Roger Perry, Barry Anderson, Maggie Meyer, Rudy Hasl, Tina Short, Frank Hamsher, Jim McLeod, Mimi Hirshberg, Polly O'Brien, Sue Schlichter, Jerry Dobson, Mary Ann Wymore, John Weil, Ed Soule, Mary Ellen Finch, Howard Gardner, Roland Barth, and my 1st grade teacher, Helen Mayfield. I also appreciate the major distractions in my life, including, but not limited to, my basketball-playing buddies and book group.

At ASCD, I offer special appreciation to Kathy Checkley, John Checkley, Scott Willis, and Genny Ostertag, my editor. I first came to know Kathy and John when they filmed a video to accompany my book *Becoming a Multiple Intelligences School*. I came to enjoy and respect them as colleagues. Scott deserves credit for helping me move this book from a vision to reality. His skill and encouragement have been invaluable. With a deft hand, Genny suggested, clarified, and molded.

Lastly, thanks go to my family members for their support. My mother, my wife, and my two standard poodles—Rita, Karleen, Casper, and B.J.—know that even though my name is on the cover of this fancy book, it's just me.

Introduction

Strong leaders are artists. They inspire, applaud, chastise, steer, and stand on the side. They create, monitor, reinforce, encourage, and stand in the back. Yes, sometimes they stand in front, too. They recognize that it is their responsibility to help create a setting in which each individual can flourish and everyone can grow. Strong leaders understand that leadership is about relationships.

Strong leaders are artists because they recognize that there is no one formula, no particular policy, no set of procedures that will always work with everyone or, even, will always work with any one person. Each unique situation and every idiosyncratic individual must be appreciated. We know that we must take a developmental approach to how our students learn; we also know that they learn best when they learn constructively, by creating their own meaning. It is no different for our teachers. They, too, must be viewed developmentally; they, too, learn best constructively. I believe that this is true of leaders and followers everywhere, in all settings, and I am sure that it is even more true of leaders in schools.

As I write this introduction, I am nearing my 28th year of leading a school. This longevity means that I have made many mistakes. I hope that I have learned from these mistakes. I certainly don't lack opportunities to learn, those times when I look back and see what I should have done differently or what I should do in the future. Just last week, for example, an entire inservice day was allocated for teachers to meet individually with administrators to discuss their professional goals. The day consisted of a series of 30-minute meetings, one after the other, after the other. I was beat at the end of the day, but I was also invigorated. It was exciting to hear the teachers' plans and to have an uninterrupted half hour to talk and learn with each of them. At the end of the day, all I could think was, *Why didn't I do this before?*

This book capitalizes on my experiences, what worked and what didn't, and offers ideas and examples for how a school can be led. I also e-mailed many educators around the world and asked for their thoughts on the issues I was addressing. You'll see many of their comments in the margins of these pages. Leadership is an art, so there are no formulas. Instead, chapters deal with the day-to-day stuff that administrators live and breathe: running meetings, evaluating teachers, working with parents, building a team, supervising projects, focusing on diversity, and encouraging collegiality.

I believe that the challenges facing school leaders are greater than those facing leaders in other arenas. This stems from the nature of education and how our schools are organized. Three particular challenges quickly come to mind.

• *Balancing measurement tensions.* In for-profit organizations, the outcomes are agreed upon and the bottom line is very clear. Educators, however, continue to debate how to measure success in schools. Should individual students, groups of students, or an entire school be evaluated only on the basis of standardized tests? What about *primarily* on standardized tests? What aspects of student growth aren't captured by any standardized test? Does "adequate yearly progress" offer a more realistic picture of what we can expect from our students and ourselves? How can PEPs (projects, exhibitions, and presentations) and portfolios be used to gauge student growth? Can these measures be used to accurately gauge teacher effectiveness?

> Throughout this book you'll find leadership advice from educators around the world.
>
> ---
>
> We are all leaders, and we are all learners.
>
> ~Tamala

Even though debates continue to rage about the validity of such instruments, and perceptive educators realize that objective tests capture only slices of a student's growth, principals are held accountable for the performance of their schools on standardized measures. Principals must focus their energies and those of their staffs on what is being measured, regardless of any misgivings they might hold about the limitations of the measurement tools. But it is not this simple. At the same time, principals must also realize that other issues are critically important to student and faculty growth and development.

• *Herding cats.* Leading teachers has been likened to conducting a symphony orchestra, coaching a basketball team, or herding cats. A conductor works at getting each member of the orchestra to play an instrument in concert with all the other members; success is determined by how well they play together. A basketball coach creates relationships in which players feed off one another and adjust to the changing tempo of the game; success is determined by how well they play together. Good leadership enables the players, whether in the orchestra or on the basketball team, to achieve more as members of the group than they ever could as individuals. A cat herder keeps the goal in mind and recognizes that it will never be easy; he often asks himself, "Why am I doing this?"

Leadership never is easy, and it's even harder to lead the kinds of people we want to teach our students. That is because many of the qualities that are found in wonderful teachers—passion, creativity, and a thirst for independence—can make it difficult for them to share, to work toward a common goal, and to be good teammates. This tendency is exacerbated because teaching is often a very autonomous activity (it shouldn't be, of course, and that is the focus of much of this book). Indeed, it can sometimes be hard for teachers to accept the fact that they have a *boss.*

For talented teachers, teaching is an art and they are artists. When I think of these teachers, I use Michelangelo as my avatar. We want Michelangelos teaching our children, yet Michelangelos are often difficult, recusant, and quite independent, and they can be difficult to lead. We must find ways to lead that inspire and challenge as well as direct and support. Supervising Michelangelo is no small task.

• *Being caught in the middle.* Principals answer to just about everyone. Officially, they are responsible to a superintendent and assistant superintendents. They are also, officially or otherwise, responsible to associate superintendents, assistants to the superintendent, deputy superintendents, area superintendents, directors of education, and curriculum directors. Let's not forget board of education members, who sometimes have difficulty recognizing what is policy and what is administration. Clearly, principals have multiple official bosses. (Some principals would add that they are responsible to the director of transportation or the director of building and grounds!)

Principals are also responsible to their teachers, who play the role of unofficial bosses. Leading schools involves creating an environment in which everyone grows, including the teachers and the principal. In that environment, principals listen to teachers, and listening implies a willingness to respond. In addition, some teachers will have more experience and clout with parents (or maybe with people who work in the central office) than does the principal. Unhappy teachers can rally parents; satisfied teachers can quell them. Teachers' unions have also given teachers a strong voice in many management issues.

Of course, principals also answer to parents. Three unhappy parents can cause a revolt. Two dissatisfied parents can create endless headaches. One malcontent parent can get an audience with the superintendent. And as any principal knows, critical and unhappy parents will be found in every school, no matter

> Leaders challenge,
> but they do not
> overwhelm. ~Nelly

the quality of the school or the skill level of the principal. Principals must work to educate and include all parents.

These unique challenges endemic to leading a school—the debate over how student and school progress can be measured, the issue of teachers as artists, and the visible and vulnerable nature of the role of the school leader—take us to one inescapable conclusion: *Leadership is about relationships.* Indeed, sometimes those relationships are quite close and intimate; at other times, they extend across countries and continents. The quotes that you see in the margins of this book, for example, are from educators around the world. Although I personally know some of these individuals, the majority are people with whom I've had "only" an ongoing e-mail relationship. Nevertheless, these are educators from whom I have learned.

Good leaders embrace these challenges and move schools forward. Whether a school is progressing from struggling status to acceptable or going from acceptable to good or moving from good to great, leadership is the key variable in its evolution.

Leading a School

Good leaders change organizations; great leaders change people. People are at the heart of any organization, particularly a school, and it is only through changing people—nurturing and challenging them, helping them grow and develop, creating a culture in which they all learn—that an organization can flourish. *Leadership is about relationships.*

Leaders increase a group's productivity by helping everyone in the group become more effective. Whatever the task or goal, a great leader helps everyone improve. A leader begins by setting the vision but doesn't stop there. A leader listens, understands, motivates, reinforces, and makes the tough decisions. A leader passes out praise when things go well and takes responsibility and picks up the pieces when things fall apart. *Leadership is about relationships.*

Leaders don't lead by issuing mandates. Leaders communicate well and often, and they listen to others. Listening doesn't mean abdicating responsibility or failing to play a leadership role. Listening means incorporating others' ideas and talents and energies into forging a vision. Sometimes leadership is obvious, but that is not always so. As Dwight D. Eisenhower observed, "Leadership is the art of getting someone else to do something you want done because he wants to do it." Good leaders bring out the best in others. *Leadership is about relationships.*

Academicians often distinguish between leadership and management. Leadership, they say, is creating the vision, dealing with those outside the organization, and inspiring others.

Management is executing the vision, dealing with employees, and maintaining standards. Perhaps some leaders don't manage, but that is not my experience. The strong leaders I've known were strong because they could lead *and* manage. Yes, leaders do create the vision, deal with external parties, and inspire. But leaders also execute the strategies that make the vision a reality, deal with the employees, and follow through to ensure that the right things are done in the right way. *Leadership is about relationships.*

Lessons Learned the Hard Way

In more than a quarter-century of running schools and trying to be a leader, I've learned some painful and powerful lessons. Four of them in particular stick with me (and, believe me, I haven't mastered these lessons yet).

Leading Nonpublic Schools

The heads of charter, parochial, and private schools deal with the same tensions as their public school peers. Their titles may be different. Instead of being the principal, they may be called the president, director, executive director, headmaster, headmistress, or head of school. But the issues they face are the same. Measurement issues are no less relevant in nonpublic schools. One difference is that there is less of a hierarchy to which nonpublic school leaders must respond, but this doesn't mean that governance is easier. Nonpublic schools will typically have boards of directors of between 12 and 25 members.

Leaders of nonpublic schools also live with an additional dose of reality. There is no higher degree of accountability than that which comes from parents deciding each year whether to continue enrollment at a particular school. When parents vote with their feet like this, their actions represent a powerful evaluation of the school. Further, when tuition is charged, the money spent often results in even higher expectations on the part of families. Of course, most nonpublic schools, charters excepted, are able to select their students and can operate with far more flexibility than their public counterparts. Perhaps the biggest difference is that most non-public school leaders have the additional responsibilities of marketing and fund-raising.

1. *Be inclusive:* All of us are smarter than any of us.

2. *Be clear:* Is it your decision, my decision, or our decision?

3. *Be fair to yourself and others:* Know the difference between excellence and perfection.

4. *Be someone who makes a difference:* Why do you want to lead a school?

Lesson 1: Be Inclusive

Warren—tall and thin and always frowning—came into my office, unannounced. My heart skipped a beat when I saw him because I knew that I would quickly be on the defensive. Warren did that to me just about every time we talked. He was the parent of two of my students, a 2nd and a 4th grader, and he always brought me criticisms and complaints. In my few months as principal, Warren had become my nemesis.

"Do you have a minute?" he asked. Honestly, I didn't have a minute. I was busy. And even if I did have a minute, the last thing I wanted to do was spend it talking to Warren.

"Of course!" I replied, and I offered him a seat anyway.

It was my first year as a principal, and I already knew that I didn't like having Warren as my chief critic. My inner-suburb school of 400 students was, according to the district's terminology, "underachieving." That meant the majority of our students were doing poorly on standardized tests. Many students came from families that qualified for free or reduced-price lunch, but I knew that wasn't an excuse. My eyes were wide open when I took the job. I understood the challenges that awaited me and was, in fact, eager to face them. The day Warren came into my office, many issues were already clear to me: Students were not learning; parents were not involved; and faculty members were doing what they had done for years, even though it wasn't effective.

"I want to see our school's standardized test scores," Warren said. "I don't want to see individual student scores, but the superintendent tells me you're here to turn things around, and I want to know what the problem is. Why do we need you?"

Leadership happens at many levels and comes from many individuals. If you've forgotten that, you're no longer a part of that leadership. ~Ben

Warren's children did well in school, so he had no data to suggest other children weren't doing just as well. In addition, a finalist for my position was a teacher at the school, someone Warren liked. Naturally, Warren was suspicious of me and questioned why I was given the job. Naturally, I was suspicious of him, too.

Warren's request was a tricky one. Schoolwide and grade-level test averages were not made public in those days. Parents knew how well their children performed on tests, teachers knew how well the grade in which they taught fared, and principals knew how grades and schools compared to one another, but that was it. The data were hierarchically bound; the information simply wasn't shared. As a result, I had a problem. I knew that I could stand behind district policy and not share the information, but doing so would alienate Warren. (It would also leave unanswered his question of why I had been hired.) On the other hand, I knew that I could ignore the policy by bringing Warren into my confidence and letting him see how our grades compared to national standards. Doing so might make Warren my ally (and answer his question of why I had been hired), but there was a risk involved with sharing the data. The two choices were pretty simple and clear.

I blew it.

I didn't share the information with Warren. As I anticipated, this refusal did not help our relationship or our level of trust. I could live with that. What I didn't expect, and this is why I blew it, was that he took my reluctance to share information and to treat him like an ally to mean that I wasn't on his side—the side of improving kids' education. Because of this, Warren became my biggest adversary when I began to make changes at the school, when I tried to get teachers to look differently at curriculum and instruction, and when I tried to increase teachers' interactions with their students' parents. He assumed, without any data to suggest otherwise, that I was trying to change things just to show that I was in charge. Or maybe he felt that I was trying

A true leader not only leads the way and gives you direction. He or she must walk side by side with you to encourage, support, listen, and learn from others. ~Estella to change things because I thought these poor kids and parents needed a white guy to show them the way. When I took the job, I realized race might be an issue because the student body was all black and I was white.

A few of my teachers complained to Warren about some of the things that I was doing (initiating weekly faculty meetings, meeting monthly with teachers about their students), and he was outraged. He led a group of parents to oppose me. The situation became very contentious and resulted in the superintendent mediating a meeting with a dozen parents and me. They had a list of concerns about me, and I responded, point by point. The superintendent shared some of the district's standardized test data, illustrating just how much my school needed to improve. That meeting was a turning point because it allowed me not only to explain what I was trying to do, but also to share my rationale about why it needed to be done.

This story ends reasonably well. By the end of my second year, well after the parent meeting, Warren had become my supporter. The more he knew of the challenges that I faced and the more he understood that we shared the same goals, the more he trusted my motives. By the end of my third year, with his help and the efforts of some talented and hardworking teachers, our students' standardized test scores improved significantly. Our scores on the reading, language, and math tests were above grade level in 14 of 15 measures for grades 1–5. Warren and I became friends of sorts, as I came to respect him for his high standards and commitment to everyone's children, not just his own. I've heard that he says similar positive things about me. My first years were not easy times, however, and I was a big part of the problem.

To this day, I frequently look back on that interaction with Warren with regret. Had I responded differently when he asked to see our grade-level average scores, how much more quickly would our school have turned around? How many sleepless nights would I have avoided, and how many difficult meetings would never have taken place? In retrospect, I realize that I missed an opportunity to create an ally by letting Warren see that I was part of the solution. Instead, I persisted in trying to solve a problem that he didn't know existed.

Even worse, although I changed schools and a variety of different issues came into play, this kind of mistake is one that I've made again and again. Simply put, on too many occasions I've failed to realize that the group is always stronger than the individual, that a principal cannot be successful without the support of parents and teachers. My progression has been slower than I'd like, and I'm sure that I'm not *there* yet. However, I now understand the importance of taking the time and expending the effort to get everyone (or almost everyone!) to agree on the problem and to work to be part of the solution. I've learned that it's not enough for me to diagnose the problem and create the strategies, even if my diagnosis is correct and my strategies are promising. After all, how willing are people to change their behaviors and do things differently if they don't accept the fact that there is a problem or a goal that needs addressing in the first place? I've learned that it is far better to involve others at the beginning, to allow them to work with me in identifying and then pursuing a common goal. That process takes longer and is often messier, but it increases the likelihood that the goal will be achieved.

> Good leaders need to be good followers.
>
> ~Duane

Lesson 2: Be Clear

This lesson is simple, yet it is a difficult one to achieve. Leaders, especially principals, get into trouble when they're not clear to others or to themselves about who gets to make what decisions. It's easy for principals to assume that everyone belongs to one big happy family, that everyone has input on all decisions, and that consensus rules the day. We all like to think that everyone shares the same perceptions and values, so everyone will choose the same decision (the decision that we'd choose, of course!). We are often tempted to leave things a bit fuzzy, to not make clear who gets to decide, and to let others believe that the decision is theirs. Teachers come to think that the opportunity to provide input is the same as getting to decide. When this happens, the seeds for conflict are planted.

Yes, there are times when principals need to make the difficult decision and assert their positional power, even though it may make others, mostly teachers, unhappy. That is part of an administrator's territory. Teachers may not be pleased with either the decision or the process, but they generally understand that this is the administrator's job. They may groan or be unhappy, but they go along with the decision. "No way would I want your job" is a comment I often hear after making a tough decision (even from those who disagree with my position).

However, making this same decision after allowing, or even encouraging, teachers to think that the decision belongs to them creates major difficulties. Teachers who believe that a decision is theirs to make only to learn later that, guess what, it's really not theirs after all will be unhappy. No, make that *very* unhappy. And who can blame them? Whether or not teachers are displeased with the decision, they will feel used and compromised.

> True leaders are respected, not circumvented.
> ~Laurie

The principal, of course, didn't intend to do that at all. She respects her teachers. She was trying to reach consensus and thought that by giving the teachers input into the decision, they would feel empowered. Her assumption was that the teachers would make the same decision that she would make and that they would all arrive at the same decision point without her having to exert any hierarchical power.

Conflict arises when teachers feel that they have been given the license to make a decision but then come to a different conclusion than the principal expects or finds acceptable. The principal backs away from giving the teachers the decision; they find the rug pulled out from under them. What began as an inclusive effort by the principal backfires. Teachers are unhappy and, even worse, no longer trust the principal.

I've come to refer to this as the "your decision, my decision, our decision" dilemma. Within a school, decisions fall in each of these areas. From the principal's perspective, "your decision" refers to those questions that are decided by teachers; "my decision" refers to those decided by the principal, alone; "our decision" refers to those that are reached collaboratively, with the principal and teachers working together. Most of the time, it's very clear who should make which decision. But most of the time is not all of the time. There are also some gray areas in which decisions aren't as clear. In these cases, teachers could make the decision, but so could the principal, or perhaps the decision could be made collaboratively. Again, what often happens is that in an effort to flatten the hierarchy and promote the "we're all on the same team" philosophy, principals are not clear ahead of time about who will decide which issues.

As tricky as this "your decision, my decision, our decision" dilemma can be, it can almost always be avoided when principals make clear who is responsible for the decision. To promote this understanding, I've found it effective to use the "your decision, my decision, our decision" terminology with my faculty. When I do so, I use it to explain an issue and to share how I have to guard against my tendency not to be as clear as I should. I'll sometimes tell a committee, "This is a 'your decision.' Whatever you decide will be fine with me." Or perhaps I'll say, "I want to hear your thoughts, but be aware that this is a 'my decision' issue. I am accountable for it and have to make the decision. Although I really do want your input, know in advance that it's ultimately my call."

I've found that teachers view this type of explicit communication as comforting. It allows them to know their role and thus reduces the likelihood that they will waste time or be overly disappointed if a decision is not to their liking. Administratively, this model helps me, too, because it forces me to plan ahead and think about what kind and degree of involvement is important. Then I can solicit input as needed. I avoid falling into the trap of soliciting input because I want to get everyone on board, even though I already know what decision I want to make.

Lesson 3: Be Fair to Yourself and Others

The speaker paused, and the room filled with principals fell silent. Adam, a high school principal, had hit a nerve deep within each of us, and we were lost in reverie and reflection. The topic was "How I manage stress in my life," and Adam was one of four principals on a panel at the principals' conference. I was also a speaker. We were to share our wisdom with the 25 or 30 other principals. The first three panelists offered the typical nostrums, myself included. One spoke of getting up early to run several times each week, another talked about making time for her family, and I talked about being sure that I have time to read and write. The audience, unusually polite for a group of educators, was quiet and attentive despite the lack of any information that would actually help manage stress. And then it was Adam's turn to speak.

"I try to understand the difference between excellence and perfection," he said.

After pausing for a moment, he went on, "At my school, we have a problem with getting the students to put the lunchroom trays back where they belong after they finish eating. This is a big issue for me, and—" He was interrupted by a few chuckles and some eye-rolling. He indignantly slammed his hand on the table. "It *is* a big deal!" he exclaimed, reacting to the audience and raising his voice. The group grew quiet.

"You see," he continued, a bit defiantly, "my students are affluent and mainly white. The cafeteria staff are all black and predominately female. It's important that our students learn the responsibility that they have to others, and cleaning up after themselves is an important part of that. I can get 90 to 95 percent of the students to put their food trays away each day, and that is excellent. But I want *perfection*. I want every student, 100 percent of the students, to put the trays away. It's only right!"

He hesitated and took a deep breath. "But I've learned that in seeking to get 100 percent of the food trays put away, I not only turn the school into a prison and drive everyone crazy, I

Good leaders are always in the quest of improving and are not scared of other people knowing more than they do. ~Nelly create an unbelievable amount of stress for myself. So I try to be realistic. *I try to understand the difference between excellence and perfection.*" He paused while our thoughts drifted to our own schools. His point was about far more than cafeteria trays. He was really talking about the need that each of us has to be realistic about what is possible, to set goals that are ambitious but achievable, and to recognize and be pleased when the glass is nine-tenths full instead of seeing it as one-tenth empty.

Alas, I am much better at talking and writing about balancing excellence and perfection than actually doing it. I can find numerous occasions when I've not been satisfied with excellence (accepting "good" wasn't even an option) and wanted perfection. Worse, I've not only wanted perfection, I've wanted it more quickly. Of course, with this kind of mind-set, there is no perfection. Even if perfection is realized, expectations increase. It becomes easy to take a major accomplishment and make it a routine expectation. This is true in every line of work and on virtually every issue; people who run schools do not have a monopoly on this problem. Yet schools are hotbeds in the search for excellence. After all, however well our students do, they can always do better! Even if we're not looking for *better*, we can always look for *more*. Each year we add programs, curriculum, and responsibilities. We celebrate our successes by setting higher and more ambitious goals for the following year, not by relishing our achievements. Then we wonder why the stress level in schools is so high.

"Excellence versus perfection" has become a common phrase among members of my administrative team and faculty. Saying these three words is a shorthand way of reminding ourselves to step back and question our assumptions and our goals. When, after all, is "good" good enough?

This issue has always been present in schools, but it is even more pronounced in our era of high-stakes testing and public accountability. In some areas, we shouldn't be satisfied with

> I love it when folks in leadership roles make themselves vulnerable and show their human side. ~Anne

"good," whereas in others, "average" is just fine, thank you. All of us, but especially school leaders, need to step back and be sure that when we seek perfection and are not willing to settle for excellence, we do so consciously and wisely. Stress flows downhill. Unless we are careful, our own ever-increasing expectations can have a pernicious effect on us and everyone around us.

Lesson 4: Be Someone Who Makes a Difference

With a few years under my belt as principal at my first school, this was the question put to me: "Why *do* you want to be a principal?" I gulped and felt the perspiration rolling down my forehead. It was 4:30 p.m. on a Thursday, and I was standing in a room in front of 30 to 40 parents and a few faculty members. You see, I had applied for a new job, to head New City School, and I was a finalist for the position. As part of the selection process, I was answering questions at a parent meeting held after school. There were scores of unknown faces in front of me, people wanting to know more about me, parents who were going to pass judgment on whether they thought that I should lead their children's school. It felt a bit like a press conference, minus the flashes from cameras. I was definitely on the spot.

"I want to be a principal," I responded, "because I want to be able to make a difference in kids' lives." I paused, warming up to the question, and then responded with vigor.

"I have been a teacher, and I loved it," I said. "I wasn't a perfect teacher, but it was really gratifying to see my students' smiling faces and watch them learn to do things that they didn't think were possible. I went home each evening feeling tired but also feeling that my efforts were worthwhile." There were some smiles in the audience, and the faculty members who were present nodded in appreciation and empathy.

"But after a number of years, even though I still was far from being a perfect teacher, I became antsy. To be candid, I grew frustrated. I worked for four principals who were good and

> Good leaders realize which decisions need to be top-down and which need to be hashed out by the group. ~Lucie

caring people but who didn't seem to understand how schools should function and be organized." At this, I noticed some quizzical looks from people in the audience.

"By that," I continued, "I mean that these principals were disciplinarians and schedulers. The schools ran well, but the principals didn't give any real attention to me or to my teaching. Curriculum and instruction simply weren't priorities of theirs. As long as I wasn't causing a problem, as long as there were no student behavior issues or complaints from parents, as long as my kids did well on standardized tests, they left me alone. No attempt was made to help me learn from senior, more experienced, and better teachers; nothing was done to enable me to work with or help new teachers. This hands-off attitude applied to the other teachers as well, and that is a shame."

I was on a roll, talking about an issue that made me passionate. I gestured toward the teachers who were standing in the audience. "However good they are," I said, "they can be better, and the job of a principal is to help that happen." One of the teachers caught my eye, smiled, and gave me a thumbs-up signal. I remember being elated when I saw that.

At this point, a man in the audience raised his hand. When I called upon him, he asked, "Do you want to be a superintendent?"

"No," I replied. "Although a superintendent influences far more students, his or her influence on any one student is significantly less. Conversely, teachers have the most influence, but it's with far fewer kids. A principal has the best of both worlds. I thought this was the case before I first became a principal, and now, having run a school for three years, I'm even more convinced that this role is one in which I can make a difference. At least that is the way it seems to me."

The question-and-answer session lasted for nearly 90 minutes. I don't remember what else was asked of me, but I must have answered reasonably well because I was offered the job. (I accepted and still work there today.) My answer to this question has remained with me, and I have thought of it many times over

Staff need to see that the leader not only directs the work, but also shares in the responsibility for getting it done. ~Rich the years. Being a principal is not an easy job, but it is a job in which one can make a difference in children's lives and, by extension, in the world. I still go home tired, and I still feel frustrations at both the things I cannot control and those things that I can control but don't. But I go to work each morning feeling good about my role.

This story is unlike the other lessons that I offer in this chapter. In the other examples, I learned from my mistakes. (OK, I tried to learn from my mistakes.) I didn't commit an error in this example, but it's an important story for me because it reminds me of why I still run a school after all these years. Like any school leader, I've had my bad days and I've had my successes. I've worked a bit in higher education, teaching classes in school administration as well as directing and teaching in a program for nonprofit management. I enjoyed all of it, but there is something special about leading a school, about making a difference in the lives of students and teachers. When I get tired and frustrated and discouraged—and, believe me, I do get tired and frustrated and discouraged—I think back to that parent "press conference" so many years ago. That memory reminds me of why I do what I do and why I enjoy it so. This lesson may be the most powerful lesson of all.

2 Promoting Collegiality

Much of my thinking about supervision and leadership stems from the work of Roland Barth. In his book *Improving Schools from Within* (1990), Barth maintains that faculty collegiality is the most important factor in determining the success of a school. The premise of collegiality is simple yet powerful: If students are to grow and learn, the adults in the school must grow and learn, too. This understanding has had a profound effect on me. When a school is alive with collegiality, then creativity and passion thrive, and every teacher improves each year. That is a lofty claim but not an unreasonable one. Collegiality has that much power!

An environment that promotes growth has never been more needed than in today's high-pressure educational world. As expectations rise and demands for accountability increase, faculty collegiality is an integral tool for developing teachers and for creating a milieu that supports their growth. Although the kinds of missions and pedagogical approaches found in schools vary dramatically—from following the thinking of E. D. Hirsch to that of Howard Gardner, for example—the quality of teachers is the key factor in students' success in every setting. As a result, regardless of mission or focus, I cannot imagine a good school in which collegiality is not an important part of the culture.

Collegiality is distinct from both congeniality and collaboration, though the terms have much in common and are often confused. Congeniality is present when people get along well and like one another. Congeniality is evidenced by smiles, laughter, and concern for others' personal lives. People ask "How was your weekend?" because they truly care. This type of interaction is meaningful because we all want to enjoy work and to know that our peers care for us. We cannot overlook the importance of congeniality because it is the base upon which collegiality is built. Indeed, it is difficult to imagine how collegiality could flourish in a school without congeniality. However, congeniality alone is not sufficient. People will not work well as colleagues simply because they enjoy and care for one another.

Collaboration has much in common with collegiality. Both terms imply a setting in which people work as colleagues and benefit from their relationships. Collaboration implies working with others, being teammates, and perhaps sharing ideas. It does not, however, focus on learning with and from one another, and that is what distinguishes it from collegiality.

Barth's collegiality contains four components specific to schools: teachers talking together about students, teachers talking together about curriculum, teachers observing one another teach, and teachers teaching one another. Despite its encompassing scope and power, Barth's model does not explicitly address the essential collegial relationship between administrators and teachers. As a result, I add a fifth component of collegiality: teachers and administrators learning together.

These kinds of collegial interactions foster reflection and dialogue, and the norm becomes a culture in which people willingly learn with, learn from, and teach their colleagues. How collegiality is manifested varies with the educational setting and context, but some commonalities apply to all situations. Figure 1 on p. 22 describes each of the components of collegiality.

The job is too hard to do alone. ~Tamala

Finding Ways to Attain Collegiality

As Lao-tzu said, "A journey of a thousand miles must begin with a single step." A setting in which teachers and administrators work as colleagues—and one in which every teacher grows—

Figure 1

The Five Components of Collegiality

1. Teachers talking together about students
- discussing students' strengths
- discussing students' needs
- discussing how students have changed over time
- comparing and contrasting how students perform in different settings
- discussing how to work with families to help students grow

2. Teachers talking together about curriculum
- developing curriculum
- reviewing curriculum
- revising curriculum
- aligning curriculum to standards
- applying multiple intelligences theory to curriculum
- integrating curriculum through thematic instruction
- designing assessment tools that teach and evaluate
- talking about pedagogy

3. Teachers observing one another teach
- gaining an appreciation for other teachers within the building
- asking questions that cause the teacher being observed to reflect
- giving positive feedback so that the teacher being observed can grow
- giving negative feedback so that the teacher being observed can grow
- sharing ideas through watching one another teach

4. Teachers teaching one another
- sharing expertise about curriculum, pedagogy, and child development
- sharing knowledge about curriculum
- sharing awareness and knowledge from readings
- sharing insights about families
- sharing what was learned from attending presentations and conferences

5. Teachers and administrators learning together
- talking about educational philosophy and school vision
- reviewing common perspectives and goals
- tackling issues and problems in a collegial manner
- discussing how individuals see issues differently due to their professional roles
- working together on faculty committees and ad hoc groups to reflect on the past and plan for the future

Components 1–4 are adapted from Barth (1990).

does not come to life quickly or easily. Creating such an environment requires vision, energy, and tenacity on the part of the school leader. Some approaches increase both the likelihood and pace of creating a collegial setting. The following strategies will help leaders who want to encourage collegiality in their schools.

Form a Book Group

The easiest way to begin to develop collegiality is by forming a book group. The group should meet voluntarily, before or after school or in the evening. The principal initiates the group and facilitates the first meeting, after which facilitation responsibilities are rotated among the participants. Whether reading a book such as *Emotional Intelligence* or an article from the latest issue of *Educational Leadership* or *Education Week*, there is much to be gained from being involved in an educational discussion while sitting on a couch or around a table.

More participation is always better, but a book group can begin with as few as four or five members. Over time, as the participants share what they learn and how enjoyable they find the discussions, the numbers will grow. Because the group is voluntary, there will be a significant number of people who cannot or choose not to attend. That is OK. If you wait for everyone to get on board, you'll never begin. A nucleus of teachers spreading the word about this positive experience will entice others to join.

> Together we are a collection of knowledge and experiences that reach beyond what any of us could be on our own. ~Ben

The principal's attendance is not an option, however. She needs to be present at the sessions and participate in the give-and-take. She needs to be a colleague who is learning, not an administrator observing. This sets the tone for future discussions and debates. Indeed, the relationships that develop from interactions in the book group make it easier for participants to talk about contentious issues and topics throughout the year, whether in the teachers' lounge or at a faculty meeting.

We have offered book groups for years at New City School, almost every summer and often during the school year. The following books have been read and discussed in faculty book groups: *Frames of Mind; The Unschooled Mind; Emotional Intelligence; Warriors Don't Cry; I Know Why the Caged Bird Sings; White Teacher; Why Are All the Black Kids Sitting Together in the Cafeteria?; Daughters; Boys and Girls Learn Differently; A Mind at a Time;* and *The No. 1 Ladies' Detective Agency.* A few teachers are almost always involved, but others choose to participate based on the book that is being discussed or what else is happening in their lives at that particular time. Providing food makes every book a bit more enjoyable.

Make Collegiality a Goal

Depending upon the teacher's skills and experience, pursuing and supporting faculty collegiality should be a stated goal. Indeed, given the importance of adult collegial learning to student learning, how could it not be? For example, a leader can focus a teacher's efforts and validate her energies by helping her set a goal of working with and learning from others. The particular strategies that are developed will, of course, frame the teacher's efforts. The teacher might agree to lead a faculty committee, help form a book group, or facilitate curriculum development for a grade level or academic department. Or the teacher might act as a mentor to a new teacher or to a teacher new to the school. Perhaps the teacher will decide to play a leadership role within a grade-level or department team. Unless collegiality becomes a part of specific goals, it will remain nothing more than rhetoric, something that is often talked about but never realized.

Develop Curriculum as Colleagues

Just as the best way to learn something is to teach it, the best way to know and understand curriculum is to develop it. Most teachers, after all, didn't choose a career in education because they wanted to become actors reading a script that was developed by others. They became teachers because they liked learning and teaching, enjoyed working with children, and wanted to use their creativity and energies in making a difference for students. Even the best curriculum is made better by educators adapting and massaging the material to fit their unique classrooms and the present year's students.

> A classroom can resemble a cave unless teachers have an opportunity to collaborate, commiserate, and contemplate with one another. Teaching is so much about human interaction, that the "other kind" of interaction, adult to adult, is critical to a teacher's feeling whole. ~Kathy

Meet to Share Ideas

Faculty meetings (discussed in Chapter 8) should be times when everyone *learns*, not just when everyone *hears*. These meetings are great opportunities for teachers to share a new technique or approach, to relate their experiences at a workshop, or to talk about a new way to assess student growth. Unfortunately, teachers are often reluctant to do this because publicly sharing a success may seem like bragging. If sharing is a part of almost every faculty meeting, however, teachers will recognize that it is simply something that everyone does, not self-promotion. When this happens, faculty meetings become productive learning sessions.

Once the norm is set for sharing successes, it also becomes much easier to share failures. It's only natural to be reluctant to share mistakes and failures, but doing so is beneficial. Sharing errors and talking about them creates an environment in which people can learn from others' mistakes. In addition, if the sharing of failures is done well, with appropriate humor and support, it can also bring a faculty closer together.

Address Collegiality on Teacher Evaluations

If we value what we measure, then a teacher's role as colleague should be addressed in the end-of-year evaluation. Indeed, if teachers are made aware that collegiality is something that will be positively considered—from listing the committees on which they have participated to noting the presentations they have given to recounting their roles in helping others grow—it will make a difference in their attitudes and actions. This is not to say that teachers will work as colleagues solely because it might be noted on their annual evaluations. But including collegiality on the annual evaluation reminds everyone that this area is important and legitimizes spending energies toward developing it.

Even if a school does not have the latitude or desire to use performance pay to link collegiality activities to remuneration, think of the effect that the following narrative would have on Irene Jones when she receives her annual evaluation: "Irene is to be commended for her efforts with a new teammate. She has led by example, inviting her new teammate to observe and critique her. She has also led by brainstorming, meeting after school on a regular basis to talk about big and little issues. Her teammate has had a good first year with us, and I know that Irene's skills and energies were instrumental in this success." Collegiality should not be all that is addressed on Irene's evaluation, of course, because collegiality reflects only a portion of her role as teacher. But collegiality is too important a portion of teachers' professional lives to be ignored.

Involve Teachers in Hiring

Including teachers in the hiring of colleagues is a wonderful way to develop and reinforce collegiality. In the first place, it's appropriate for teachers to have some input in determining with whom they will work. Second, participation in the hiring experience is a terrific forum for reflection and growth. Beyond the consideration of whether candidate Juan's experience outweighs candidate Janel's enthusiasm, the dialogue of the hiring process forces teachers to talk about what is important in education; what is needed in their particular school, grade, or department context; and what comprises good teaching. Lastly, because candidates meet with their prospective peers as well as the principal in the hiring process, the interview becomes an entry point to establishing peer and mentor support for the new hires.

At New City School, teachers are involved in all hiring decisions. I typically do the initial screening to reduce the field to two or three strong candidates. At that point, the potential teammates (and often a teacher or two from adjacent grades) join me for the group interview. I ask the opening question: "Pretend we haven't reviewed your résumé, and tell us about yourself." Then I mainly observe and allow the teachers to question the candidate. After the interviews, the teachers and I talk as colleagues to determine which candidate would be the best person for the position. Invariably, these discussions address the kinds of teaching qualities and skills that we seek in order to match or support the teachers on the present teaching team. We also consider how the range of life experiences that candidates possess might make them more effective teachers and teammates. This discussion is a wonderful tool for encouraging teachers' reflection.

Before the group interview, I make it clear to the teachers sitting in on the interview that I can veto the hiring of a teacher even if they, as prospective teammates, think the candidate would be great. I also note that I cannot hire someone unless they want to work with that person. This means the hiring truly is a collegial decision. Occasionally, after the interview, teachers will have trouble making a decision because of some hesitancy or a lack of information. They might say, "I'm not sure I really got to know her" or "I'd like to hear more about his approach to literacy." When this happens, I offer the teachers an opportunity to invite the candidate to meet at school or go to lunch, without an administrator's being present. After all, what better way is there for them to determine whether they seem likely to work well together than by engaging in a long lunch discussion or spending time in a classroom talking about education? Before this meeting takes place, I make it clear that I would be pleased to hire the candidate and that the decision is theirs. (Obviously, I make this offer for them to have a subsequent meeting only if I am comfortable hiring the candidate.)

Each time my teachers and a candidate meet separately after an initial interview, it is a productive experience. Often, they come away with a much better sense of the candidate and are excited about having him or her as a new teammate. I then follow up and offer the position to the candidate. Sometimes my teachers come back with the realization that the candidate would not be a good hire, and they appreciate the opportunity to learn that firsthand. *Always* they come back grateful for the

> Children learn how to be team players by observing team players. ~Debbie

opportunity to get to know a prospective teammate and to have such strong input in the hiring process. Sharing the responsibilities for hiring increases the likelihood that there will be a good match among the teachers, something particularly important in a collegial setting. Sharing the hiring process is also a powerful way of showing teachers that they are trusted. Prospective teachers, too, receive a powerful message about trust and the type of school at which they hope to work.

The following events happened last summer. A teaching team and I interviewed a candidate, and it was clear that she had rich experiences and many talents. What was less clear to her potential teammates—and to her—was the quality of the "fit." How well would she work as a member of a four-person team? After the team interview, the teachers wondered how receptive she would be to their ideas and how much respect she would have for what they had built. When I talked with the candidate, she had many of the same questions and wondered if the team would be open to her ideas. Everyone agreed that it was difficult to make an assessment about something as amorphous as teaming ability in a brief interview, so the teachers and the candidate were quite pleased when I suggested a second, longer, and more casual visit. They met in a classroom without me. The story ends well: The candidate and teachers agreed that it would be a good match. Of course, the story would have ended well even if they had not agreed. In either case, the protagonists would have obtained valuable information and each of them would have played an important part in the process.

A caveat to consider when involving teachers so intimately in the hiring process is that we all tend to see merit in and are attracted to people who remind us of ourselves. This predisposition is even more true when we are considering those who might be our coworkers and teammates. As a result, it is only natural for teachers to want to work with others who share their attitudes and hold their values. That similarity can certainly reduce possibilities for conflict and increase the likelihood for congenial relationships that might lead to collegiality. However, we need to be careful that a teaching team doesn't simply replicate itself in the hiring process. The tendency to want to select others who are similar can make it more difficult to increase the diversity within a faculty; it can also make it more difficult to bring in someone who will offer a unique perspective. I have found that the best way to address this tendency is to talk about it with teachers before the hiring process begins. This issue becomes part of a larger discussion on the qualities we are looking for in a new teammate.

Create Applications That Reveal

Much can be learned about a candidate from the teaching application if that is a purpose of the application. Because school cultures are different, getting a match between a candidate and a school—more properly, between a candidate and the school's faculty—is essential. It is not enough to establish that a candidate has the appropriate degree and experience, although that is necessary. We should use the application as the first step in enabling the candidate to reveal her educational philosophy and worldview. An individual school should have the option of creating its own teacher application form in addition to what is required by the district. The forms should reflect the school's mission and needs. To interview at a particular school, candidates might submit individual school applications after their general applications are screened at the district level.

At New City School, we require applicants to submit a cover letter, résumé, and references; to submit information to allow us to obtain a criminal background check; and to complete our application form. Given our mission and educational philosophy, we also ask questions that speak to multiple intelligences (MI), the role of the personal intelligences (also known as emotional

There is no greater force for professional development among school staff and, ultimately, for student learning than collegiality. Without collegiality, we're working in a vacuum and very much alone in our thinking.

~Kathleen

intelligence, or EQ), and diversity. As a result, our application form, shown in Appendix A, asks applicants to respond to three questions:

1. Are there differences between success in school and success in life?

2. Describe, as developmentally appropriate for the age of students that you would like to teach, what issues of human diversity are important and how they should be addressed.

3. What book or work of art has had the greatest impact on you?

If the culture of education is truly to change, the practice of a teacher walking into his or her classroom and shutting the door to all other adults has got to stop. ~Mike

As you can imagine, reading these responses helps us get to know the applicant and enables us to begin to make a judgment about whether this is someone who would fit well with our mission and teaching team. Many times a candidate's responses become a topic of questions and discussion at the group interview.

Though these questions yield rich insight into a person's beliefs, how a candidate responds to the small blank box on the front of our application form yields even more information (see Appendix A). The directions instruct the candidate to "Use this space as you wish, as another way to tell us, or show us, something about you. Let yourself go. Be creative. Be humorous. Be adventurous. Be serious. You decide." The range of possibilities for completing the box is almost endless.

Candidates use this space to write poems, offer quotes, or make statements (all in very small handwriting!). Sometimes they include photo collages or pictures they have drawn. Occasionally they glue three-dimensional objects to the form. In addition, a small flyer that talks about collegiality is sent to each candidate with the application form. The flyer explains why collegiality is so important to us and describes the opportunities for teachers to learn together at New City School. It is important that prospective teachers see our focus on collegiality and want to work in this kind of setting.

Valuing Emotional Intelligence

I have already noted that collegiality is built upon congeniality.
This means that leaders must work to create a school climate in
which everyone gets along. Strategies range from the simple—
periodically having food in the faculty lounge to entice teachers
to come and chat—to the complex—consciously exhorting
teachers to work on their emotional intelligence (EQ). Developing EQ (or the personal intelligences) is important because a
collegial setting requires that teachers work more closely
together than is often the case in schools. Teachers need to be
skilled in both giving feedback to and receiving it from their colleagues. This can be difficult; indeed, the very teachers who
excel in patient communication with students sometimes find it
much harder to communicate with adults. As I discuss in Chapters 7 and 8, school leaders need to emphasize improving adult-
to-adult communications.

> Through collaboration and conversation, we can teach each other so much. We are each a library of information, experiences, useful tips. ~Rachel

Administrators should make working on their personal
communication with adults a priority, too. Simply put, a leader
must form relationships that build a team. This is true in any
setting, and especially true in a collegial setting. Writing in the
Harvard Business Review, Nohria, Joyce, and Robinson (2003)
illustrate this point. The authors observe that a range of personality characteristics is not significant in a CEO, including
whether the person is "viewed as a visionary or detail-oriented,
secure or insecure, patient or impatient, charismatic or quiet."
One quality does matter: "the ability to build relationships with
people at all levels of the organization and to inspire the rest
of the management team to do the same. CEOs who present
themselves as fellow employees rather than masters can foster
positive attitudes that translate into improved corporate
performance" (p. 51). Unless principals are careful, they can
spend so much time doing the tasks that are necessary to
survive that they ignore the building of relationships that are

necessary to succeed. Some ideas about this topic are included in Chapter 7.

Similarly, in *Multiple Intelligences and Leadership* (2002), Susan Murphy talks about vision and communication.

> Most successful leaders have the ability to communicate persuasively, either through creative use of words that paint a compelling view of the future for the organization or work group, or by the certainty with which the leader introduces the mission and the strategic plans to accomplish that mission. The second potential for influence comes from a leader's ability to tune in to the needs of the followers. Those people who feel that they are truly understood may be more likely to listen to the leader's ideas and implement his or her plans. (p. 174)

Here again, school leaders need to find the time to listen to others, painful and as inefficient as that might seem. They must remember that one-way communication, by definition, is not good communication. One-way communication can relay a message, but it rarely accomplishes a task.

These are issues with which I struggle, even after more than 25 years of experience in running schools. Intellectually, I know that I need to take the time to solicit input and make sure everyone is on board. I understand that it is important for me simply to "hang out" in the teachers' lounge, no matter how deep the pile of papers, phone messages, and e-mail messages that taunts me from my desk. But this is hard to do (much harder to do than to write about!). Appropriately, Roland Barth once commented, "The obstacles to the job are the job." We all need to remember that success begins with building relationships. It doesn't end there, and relationships aren't the only things that matter. Unless the relationship piece is in place, however, successfully completing the task will be much more difficult, whatever the task may be.

Creating a Culture of Collegiality

The job of the principal is to create a school culture that transcends personality, even her own. A strong culture offers a clear sense of expectations to everyone about what is important. This includes how to teach students, as well as how to interact with other adults. In talking about culture, Deal and Peterson (2003) note that "highly respected organizations have evolved a shared system of informal folkways and traditions that infuse work with meaning, passion, and purpose" (p. 1). They also observe that "cultural patterns are highly enduring, have a powerful impact on performance, and shape the ways people think, act, and feel" (p. 4). This is especially true in schools: "In the world of education with its multiple challenges and complex goals, ritual is probably more important than in a business with a tangible product or service" (p. 32).

Together we understand; divided we just stand— if we're lucky. ~Brian

All schools have a culture, although many times we are not aware of it. A culture that is underground can foster misunderstandings and will surely fail to move the institution forward. Barth defines culture as "the complex pattern of norms, attitudes, beliefs, behaviors, values, ceremonies, traditions, and myths that are deeply ingrained in the very core of the organization" (R. S. Barth, personal communication, October 16, 2004). Barth (2002) suggests that a school's culture can be made explicit by answering the following questions:

- What are the characteristics of students who succeed?
- What are the characteristics of teachers who succeed?
- What does the principal value?
- What is the communication pattern from principal to teachers?
- What is the communication pattern from teachers to principal?

- What is celebrated at a school?
- What takes place at faculty meetings?
- What doesn't take place at faculty meetings?
- What advice do teachers new to a school need to know?

I believe that these additional questions also are relevant:

- What do we do that we should abandon?
- How do our critics view us and why?
- What institutional *old* mistakes do we continue to make?
- Under what circumstances is it OK to make mistakes?
- What new areas or directions should we pursue?
- What should we be celebrating?

Faculty collegiality happens because of our administration.
~Julie

Using these questions as "discussion starters" at a series of faculty meetings would lead to rich dialogues about values, educational philosophies, and what needs to take place to make the school better.

Growing in a Collegial Setting

Teaching can be a remarkably insular activity. In too many situations, teachers spend their day interacting with students, getting little or no feedback from other adults. We wonder why it can be difficult for teachers to continue to grow and learn, but we should not be surprised that this is the case. School settings often work against this kind of adult growth taking place.

In contrast, a collegial setting is one in which every teacher will grow. This setting attracts the teachers who make a difference in students' lives. These teachers are not necessarily more expensive, they may or may not have an advanced degree, and they may or may not be technologically savvy. They are, however, teachers who continually grow and learn. They look for creative ways to reach their students, and they look for creative ways to challenge themselves. The best way to attract and keep these teachers is to offer a setting in which collegiality is the norm. In a collegial school, everyone can flourish.

Exploring the History of Supervision

3

The model that I present describes leadership as an interactive process based on relationships and expertise. In my model, school leaders work to create settings in which everyone grows, children and adults alike. This model stems from three assumptions about people and organizations.

The first assumption is that most people desire to do a good job and want to grow. Most employees want to be able to take pride in their work. This is especially true of educators, people who have chosen to spend their careers making life better for children.

The second assumption is that organizations should be settings in which employees are both supported and challenged. Leaders need to work with their employees and support them, but leaders also must hold employees to high standards and expect that improvement will be the norm. However good employees are today, they need to be better tomorrow, next week, next month, and next year.

The third assumption is that the group is smarter than any individual. Wise leaders learn from and grow with those around them.

This leadership model may seem logical, respectful, and appropriate, but leadership has not always been viewed this way. By briefly reviewing the history and evolution of leaders in organizations, we can better understand and appreciate the implications of today's leadership models.

The Origins of Hierarchy

Organizations, hierarchies, and different models of supervision have been an essential part of the human condition for thousands of years. In *Guns, Germs, and Steel* (1999), Jared Diamond makes the case that an integral step in the evolution of society was the transition over many thousands of years from hunting-gathering to farming. Hunter-gatherers lived in small bands, roaming to find game and never settling in one place long enough to build a permanent home or create a village. As a result, they never developed the structure and organization that comes from living together over time.

Farmers, on the other hand, necessarily lived in one place for long periods. Consequently, different community roles began to evolve as people saw the efficiency that came from dividing their labor. Forms of organization evolved that capitalized on the different skills of individuals. No longer did every male in the tribe spend all his waking hours hunting game. Some still hunted for their food, but others developed crafts and sold their talents (for example, tanning hides or making pottery or shoes) in the marketplace in exchange for food.

As labor became more focused, groups of individuals working on a particular craft would join forces and physically work near one another. Over time, further delineation of responsibility occurred, with individuals becoming accountable for only a portion of a complete task or product. One person worked on one portion of an object; another person worked on another piece. A degree of coordination and organization became necessary, not just to coordinate workers' efforts and keep harmony within the group, but also to help both the individuals and the collective to become as efficient as possible.

The advent of organizations enabled the development of a series of roles and relationships in which one individual could direct another's actions in a limited realm; this was the first hierarchy. Early hierarchies were established through legacy and maintained through brute force. Nevertheless, some remarkable

> Teachers often become overburdened, especially in a small school like mine, and sometimes teachers are not good at saying no. ~Bonnie

achievements (such as the building of the Egyptian pyramids) occurred under this form of organization. Indeed, through the first thousand years A.D., the norm for large organizations, usually armies, was a hierarchy based on coercion.

This form of organization was effective, though the methods used to establish and maintain the hierarchy took a great toll on its members. That there were advantages stemming from a group of individuals organized in a hierarchy is beyond question. One need only look at the historical scorecard: Whenever a society with a hierarchy encountered a society without one, the society with the hierarchy always prevailed, often through violent means. Of course, the hierarchy itself did not determine this outcome; rather, the efficiencies and effectiveness that were the result of the hierarchy ensured success. In a hierarchy, individuals were responsible for a set skill or task, something that they could master. In a hierarchy, directions were given and followed.

The presence of organizations and hierarchies had a positive effect on almost all aspects of preparation for conflict: planning strategies, forging weapons, allocating resources, conducting war. Beyond this, as Diamond (1999) points out, living in close quarters and working in organizations also created immunity to many diseases (something that did not occur when people were predominantly hunter-gatherers). The combination of organizational effectiveness and immunity to diseases enabled a relatively few Europeans to defeat thousands of Central and South Americans in the early 1500s.

Throughout the centuries, although the names and titles varied—king, queen, emperor, empress, pharaoh—societies developed and formed around structures that afforded them advantages. True, not all segments of a society gained from these organizations. Often an underclass was subjugated and exploited. My purpose here is not to argue that organizational hierarchies were moral or fair; often they were—and are— neither. Rather, in Darwinian terms, the point is that when people came together and formed a hierarchical organization, the likelihood of that society's survival was improved.

As societies evolved, some bosses existed in the world of commerce, and the apprentice system relied on a boss-subordinate relationship. For hundreds of years, however, the only large organizations with formal, complex hierarchies were military. A boss and workers might exist on a farm or in a factory or a store, but these farms, factories, and stores remained fairly small, with little or no hierarchical structure until the assembly line was introduced to modern business.

Large organizations with true hierarchies came to prominence in the last part of the 19th century. When the scope of the task mandated it (such as building the transcontinental railroad), the model that had been used so successfully in the military was brought to the business world. Once that happened, there was no turning back. For most of the past 100 years, we have assumed that a traditional hierarchy is the most efficient and effective way to organize people in a work setting. This thinking has been embodied in the work of many leaders. Consider Frederick Taylor, who popularized the notion of scientific management at the turn of the 20th century, carefully prescribing the angle at which a shovel should go into the ground to ensure that the worker was as efficient as possible. Or recall the ultimate bureaucrat, Robert McNamara, the first president of Ford Motors not to be a member of the Ford family and the secretary of defense during much of the Vietnam War.

Efficient and effective management, however, did not mean satisfying everyone. Figure 2 summarizes these trends in management theory.

The Assumptions of Hierarchy

The assumption that hierarchies are the best way to organize a work force rests on three main principles:

1. The nature of work is predictable and constant and can be divided into discrete tasks.

2. Supervisors are more knowledgeable than their employees.

Figure 2

Management Practices Through Time

Time Period	Predominant Practice	Leading Advocates	Working Conditions
Ancient times to the 20th century	Rule by legacy and brute force	Niccolo Machiavelli, Attila the Hun	Workers were often conscripted; many working conditions were inhumane.
1900 to 1960	Scientific management, the assembly line, corporate America	Frederick Taylor, Henry Ford	Workers had little say about their jobs; decisions came from bosses "on high."
1960 to 1990	Humanistic management, Total Quality Management	W. Edwards Deming, Peter Drucker, Tom Peters	Employers listened to workers and sought their input; leaders realized that workers who feel better about their jobs will perform better.
1990 to the present	The learning organization, collegiality	Peter Senge, Roland S. Barth	Workers learn with and from colleagues; leaders must create conditions that foster growth.

Who They Are: Niccolo Machiavelli, author of *The Prince;* Attila the Hun, conqueror of much of Europe in the 5th century; Frederick Taylor, father of scientific management; Henry Ford, developer of the automobile assembly line; W. Edwards Deming, father of Total Quality Management; Peter Drucker, originator of the phrase *the knowledge worker* and author of dozens of books; Tom Peters, coauthor of *In Search of Excellence;* Peter Senge, creator of the learning organization and author of *The Fifth Discipline;* Roland S. Barth, author of *Improving Schools from Within.*

3. Supervisors have a right to direct employees; employees will unquestioningly accept direction.

For many years, these principles were accepted without challenge. Indeed, there was some veracity to such claims. Work *was* predictable and constant. Work *could* be divided into discrete tasks. Supervisors *were* more knowledgeable than their employees, and almost everyone felt that supervisors had the *right*, if not the obligation, to direct employees, who would willingly do what they were told.

Times have changed, and these hierarchical principles are no longer valid. We can debate whether or not this change is progress (my bias is that it *is*, but others may disagree), but we cannot debate the fact that in the United States, a dramatic shift has been taking place in the work environment over the past 25 years. In particular, the relationship of employees to work and employees to supervisors has changed significantly. Although education lags behind business, schools today reflect many of the changes in the business world. Let us look more closely at these principles and see why they have changed.

The Nature of Work

In the early 1900s, Henry Ford pioneered the automotive assembly line. Workers possessed, by and large, little formal education or training, and they stood in one spot and performed the same function hour after hour. This model not only created complex machinery at a relatively low price, but it was so efficient that decades later, the ability of the United States to manufacture and produce at a higher level than the rest of the world was a major factor in the triumph of the Allied Forces in World War II. The Marshall Plan rebuilt Europe around the same industrial, hierarchical model that had led to the success in the war.

After World War II, W. Edwards Deming brought a focus on statistical measures, later termed Total Quality Management, to Japanese industries. With a heavy emphasis on quality control and measurement, Japanese manufacturing companies flourished.

Education eventually adopted this mind-set (noted by Callahan in *Education and the Cult of Efficiency*, 1962). In the late 1960s and early 1970s, "teacher-proof" curriculum materials were created. They were based on the idea that if the curriculum was sufficiently delineated and scripted, then any teacher could be successful with it. Instructional models, such as Madeline Hunter's, suggested that there is a certain formula to teaching. If a teacher will simply follow that formula, success will come. Teachers' editions that accompanied textbooks contained the exact comments that teachers should make to the class, printed in red ink. These prompts ranged from "Why do you think they called it the 'New World'?" to "Turn the page now." (As humor columnist Dave Barry would say, "I am not making this up!")

When work was predictable and discrete, and when the work force was unsophisticated, there may have been merit in dividing the tasks and designing the work so that original thoughts and creative ideas were eliminated. Today, however, work is anything but predictable and constant. The electronic revolution has changed business models. Worldwide competition means that businesses must operate leaner, with fewer employees, and they must be more attuned to the marketplace than ever before. Through the Internet, almost every vendor has an opportunity to sell an item to almost every consumer; the corner paint store or drugstore no longer has a quasi-monopoly due to location or a lack of competition. The jury is still out on whether this proliferation of e-businesses will be truly advantageous to consumers, but there is no question that the Internet already has changed the way business is done.

Education is also undergoing remarkable changes. Externally, the advent of choice and consumerism in education, shown by the rapid growth of charter schools, will change the way that *all* schools operate. More charter schools will be formed, and current public schools will respond to the competition by acting more like charter schools: forming around missions, reducing central office bureaucracy, marketing their "product," and becoming more accountable. Volumes of information about a school's performance will be made available to the

It is imperative that teachers have a sense of their personal and professional mission in educating their students. The supervisor who facilitates a "head and heart" leadership approach elicits and shares in that mission.

~Mary Ann

public as schools compete with one another. More and more, schools will be judged primarily, if not only, by their students' scores on standardized tests—whether or not it is right (and I think it is not). The No Child Left Behind legislation only exacerbates this trend. As schools strive to show that they are successful in order to attract and hold their students and families, teachers' work will be anything but predictable and constant.

At the same time, internal factors will cause work to be even less predictable and constant. As anyone who has taught for a decade or longer can attest, students are changing. Many children come to school with a range of needs that is far greater than it was in the past. More children live in poverty, and family dissolution and divorce remain an issue for many children. Each of these conditions has major implications for students' readiness to learn. Attention spans and development in the personal/emotional intelligences wane as children spend hours and hours each week in front of a television or computer screen. Teachers not only must teach the three Rs and English as a second language. They also are responsible for drug education, sex education, and fostering higher-level thinking. Teachers prepare IEPs, and they work with students labeled BD, LD, ADD, ADHD, EMR, gifted, and mainstream. Sometimes, teachers walk through the same metal detectors at the doors as do the students. Here, too, the context, constantly in flux, means that the role of the teacher is anything but predictable and constant.

Even more changes are around the corner. Perhaps the biggest shift will be in how teachers execute their roles. Traditionally, schools have been *curriculum-centered*. Teachers' planning stemmed from the curriculum. A set curriculum existed, often developed by publishing companies. Teachers taught that curriculum, and students were expected to learn that curriculum. Those who did were considered smart; the rest of the students were good and nice, but they were not smart. Recently, we have witnessed a sea change in education initiated by

> Strength for the sake of power is not effective. Strength through collaboration is effective. ~Lynn

Howard Gardner's book on multiple intelligences, *Frames of Mind* (1983), and reinforced by a spate of research on brain-based learning and brain-compatible classrooms: More and more educators are creating *student-centered* classrooms.

In a student-centered classroom, planning stems from the students' needs and talents. Teachers begin by looking at each student, and then they fashion curriculum and instruction appropriately. Each child cannot have a unique learning program, but teachers can design individual plans, make accommodations, and create special learning opportunities. Basing instruction on a student's needs moves teaching further away from work that is predictable, constant, and discrete. This shift has enormous implications for how teachers work and how they are supervised.

The Knowledge of Supervisors

General educational levels have risen since the notion of hierarchy was first introduced into the workforce. A better educated workforce means that in some organizations, employees are just as likely as the boss to have an advanced degree. As Mintzberg (1998) observes, "Leadership is clearly a tricky business in professional organizations" (p. 144).

More recently, the Internet has proved to be a powerful tool for distribution of knowledge. A motivated worker can cruise among millions of Web sites to access practically any information. Many colleges and universities are offering online training, credit, and degrees. Each year, it seems the disparity between the educational level and knowledge base of supervisors and their employees gets smaller.

This disparity is even more apparent in schools. Anyone who works in a school recognizes the ludicrousness of the belief that principals are the repositories of knowledge and know more about everything than all their teachers. There is simply too much information about how students learn, along with too

Give feedback that promotes reflection and growth. ~Tamala

much content information, to allow any one individual to know it all. This doesn't even speak to the growing time demands and complexity of the principal's role, still another reason why it is naive, at best, to think that the principal knows more than her employees. Perhaps Roland Barth (1990) captures this phenomenon best when he talks of "presumed competence" in referring to school principals: "Everyone supposes we know how to do it. We get trapped into pretending we know how to do it" (p. 70).

However, as we will see, such a reality does not suggest that the principal lacks an instructional leadership role or that she cannot help her employees grow; absolutely, she can and she should. It does imply that although principals have expertise and may know more than some—maybe many—of their employees, they can no longer supervise based purely on the superiority of their expertise in curriculum and instruction.

> A wise supervisor recognizes those who need little supervision.
>
> ~Becky

The Right to Direct

Once, almost everyone felt that supervisors had the right, if not the obligation, to direct employees and that employees should willingly do what they were told. A series of events in the United States challenged this thinking, from the assassination of John F. Kennedy, to Watergate, to the Vietnam War, to the 2000 presidential election. These events have left several generations with a distrust of authority. No longer do we assume that any one individual has the "right" to tell others what to do. That shift is good and healthy, but it means that a supervisor's job is far more difficult than in the past, when unquestioning adherence to directives could be expected.

But there is more. The pervasiveness of information available through the Internet, the boundary-free nature of e-mail communications, workers' rights of all kinds, and an increasing informality in our society combine with the distrust of authority to negate much of the positional powers of bosses. A generation ago, a boss could expect an employee to do something, just because he told him to do it. Today, employee acceptance and compliance often is not based on the positional, legitimate power that bosses hold.

The Evolution of Leadership

A hierarchy in which the lines of communication were limited and the chain of command was clear and rigid was once considered the portrait of a fine organization. Today, such a hierarchy is no longer effective. As the relationships between supervisors and supervisees change, so too must the organizational structure change. In discussing today's leadership context, David Halberstam (2004) refers to "the broader, less hierarchical culture, in which you cannot give orders and assume that they will be obeyed. . . . People are better educated, and the truly talented ones, the ones you want to motivate, have many more options of their own. They're not likely to sit around and take orders from a harsh drill-sergeant-like superior" (p. 62).

> Supervisors need to be seen as partners in the educational process. ~Sister Marie

By understanding how leadership and organizational structures have evolved, we can have a better appreciation for their shape today. Again, this change is as true in schools as it is in other organizations. Societal trends and changes affect schools, and principals no longer receive the deference and respect that they used to be given based purely on their position. If I were to ask one of my talented teachers what she thinks of the idea that supervisors have the right to direct employees and that employees will unquestioningly accept direction, she would respond, without missing a beat, "Those days are long gone!" Similarly, explaining that the term *supervisor* derives from a *superior* person *viewing* another would yield laughter, at best, if shared at a faculty meeting.

Supervision as we have traditionally defined it—employees following bosses' directives because, well, because the boss was the boss—is an outmoded concept. This change does not mean that supervision cannot happen, should not happen, or does not happen. Instead, supervisors must possess the attitudes and skills that help them treat employees as talented and creative knowledge workers. Supervisors must facilitate growth and both support and challenge their employees. Supervisors must learn with and from their colleagues, as leadership is about relationships. Throughout this book, I will offer some new ways of looking at supervision, mind-sets, and strategies in which the goal is growth, not just compliance.

Setting Goals

4

If you don't know where you are going, any road will get you there. This advice, given by the Cheshire Cat to Alice as she wandered through Wonderland, captures the importance of goals. Without goals, what determines where we will spend our time or how we will focus our energies? Do we focus on developing a particular aspect of curriculum, or do we create new assessment instruments? Do we refine our questioning skills or work on our wait-time? Do we give special attention to the students who are lagging or to the ones who are blossoming? Or do we set all that aside to work on creating home-school partnerships?

A big part of the difficulty in setting and following through on professional goals is that there are so many worthy directions. Each of the activities listed above is not only needed; each also is *necessary*. How can we fail to address curriculum, pedagogy, and assessment? How can we not strive to meet the needs of all students? How can we not make the extra effort to work with parents?

But reality intrudes. We simply cannot do all these things and do them well. Finite hours and energy mean that we must prioritize and focus our efforts. If we do not, we will wander here and there, like Alice, following whims and responding to spur-of-the-moment crises. Without a focus, we are likely to spend our time heading in two directions, both counterproductive. On the one hand, we may spread our energies too widely. When this happens, we cannot achieve enough progress in any one area to make a difference for our students or to generate a sense of satisfaction for ourselves. On the other hand, we may simply continue with the same behaviors and activities of previous years, regardless of their effectiveness. Doing this is a disservice to our students and teachers (and to ourselves).

The goal-setting process can be a tool to focus ourselves and others on a path that leads to professional growth. Principals should set goals *with* their teachers, and they should set goals for themselves, which they should share with others (more on this later). The goal-setting process should be collaborative, with principals and teachers working together. Teachers live their goals, so it is logical and fair that they should have significant input in developing them. Goal setting and monitoring (henceforth whenever the term *goal setting* is used, it implies goal monitoring as well) are an integral part of professional development. After all, without goals, how will you know if you succeed?

> If you don't have that light at the end of the tunnel to strive toward, you'll never get out of the dark. ~Debbie

Too often, the goal-setting process is done poorly. We are tempted, for example, to give the most talented teachers little attention and devote most of our time and energy to newer or struggling teachers. This is a mistake. Newer and struggling teachers need attention, but the best teachers also benefit from reflection and dialogue. No matter how good they are, they can become better. It is not easy to set goals that are relevant and reasonable and that will contribute to learning. Once goals are set, it is even more difficult to monitor the process. However, given the important role that goal setting can play in professional growth, goal setting is something that must be done, and must be done well, with all our teachers.

Factors in Selecting Goals

How goals are set, their focus, and the way we monitor progress toward achieving them varies due to a host of factors. In thinking about the goal-setting process, we need to consider the teaching context:

Nonprofit Versus For-Profit Goals

Because it is so difficult to measure progress in education (some would argue that it is difficult to even define progress), the goal-setting dilemma is even more challenging in schools and other nonprofit organizations than it is in the for-profit world. After all, at the end of the year, businesses can look at their balance sheets to determine if it they were successful: Did they generate enough revenue to make a sufficient profit? Did the company generate shareholder value? In some jobs, such as sales or professional services, pay is very individualized and based solely on productivity as measured by a dollar sign.

Of course, this is not the case in education. We bridle, appropriately, at the thought of the progress of our students (or ourselves) being measured only by standardized test scores. We know that there is much more to educating students than increasing their gains on tests, important as that can be. Simply put, *all things that are important cannot be measured.* Balancing the measurable and nonmeasurable aspects of growth makes the goal-setting process more complex in schools and other nonprofit organizations.

- What are the students' needs?
- What is the school level (elementary, middle, secondary)?
- Does the school have a particular focus or direction?
- Is there a particular curriculum or pedagogical issue that is being addressed?
- Does the teacher work alone or as part of a team?
- What is the administration's philosophy on goals? Who sets them, how is goal setting done, how is progress measured, and what role does attaining goals have in how teachers are viewed or rewarded?

As important as the teaching context is to the setting of goals, so too are the talents and needs of the teacher. We should also reflect on the following:

- What is the teacher's knowledge base?
- What are the teacher's skills?
- What are the teacher's interests and passions?
- Is the teacher open to new ideas and strategies?

The combination of the teaching context and the individual's talents determines what goals are set. A new teacher in Davis, California, working with underachieving and impoverished students should have different goals than his teammate with 20 years of experience. Their goals should be different from those of a teacher in Racine, Wisconsin, who works with gifted students and was selected Teacher of the Year. Still different will be the goals of a veteran teacher in Orlando, Florida, who has a new class or is using a new mathematics curriculum. Note also that the paths to attaining goals can be radically different even if the goals are the same. There are many sound ways to pursue any goal, and the goal plan should be influenced by both the teaching context and the characteristics of the individual teacher. Irrespective of their talents and needs, all teachers prosper when they have input into their goals, when they can work from their strengths and passions, and when they learn with and from others.

The Assignment of Goals

The kinds of goals and the process for goal setting will vary with the experience and skill of the teacher. In general, it is always good to offer teachers opportunities to create their goals and ways their progress can be measured. However, there are times, especially with younger (or weaker) teachers, when an administrator needs to assign the goal.

Years ago, for example, I worked with a teacher who had many strengths but was far more negative with her students than was appropriate. We talked about this at length, yet she never quite accepted my assessment. "These are big kids," she would say, "and it's a tough world." Although I could not change her attitude, I assigned her the goal of making the feedback that she wrote on her students' papers more positive. (The good news in this story is that I monitored the student work and she did, indeed, become much more positive in the written comments that she gave to the students.)

No matter who assigns the goals, the goal-setting process should be collaborative. Who the collaborators are—a teacher and principal, two teachers, several teachers, or a group of teachers and the principal—will vary depending upon the school context, the individuals, and the goal. In all cases, the goal-setting process should include at least two people who agree on the goals and then communicate periodically to monitor progress. Sharing goals and the progress toward them increases accountability. *Goals that are not shared with others are just hopes.*

Characteristics of Goals

The factors that cause goals to differ are endless, encompassing all the different kinds of teaching situations and the differences in knowledge, skills, and attitudes among teachers. Despite these differences, however, the following elements should be part of all teacher goals.

Goals Should Be Meaningful

One might wonder why this characteristic even needs to be stated. Of course goals should be meaningful, and they should lead to increased student learning. Although learning can be defined and measured in many ways—from scores on traditional or standardized tests to rubric-based assessments of presentations to a reduction in altercations in the lunchroom—increased learning should be at the heart of all goals. But there is more to the descriptor *meaningful*.

Goals are most meaningful when their attainment benefits both students and teachers. Absolutely, the goal-setting process should benefit students; that is beyond doubt. But the goal-setting process should also benefit teachers. Unless teachers

> Accomplishing goals helps people to set more goals with ease and helps prepare them for more goal setting and achievement.
> ~Sharon

set goals for their professional development and achieve them—unless teachers also grow—their students will only make short-term, minimal gains. The goal-setting process should reflect the fact that student growth results from an interaction between student and teacher. A meaningful goal-setting process addresses the growth of both students and teachers.

The relationship between teacher and student learning is obvious, but all too often this relationship isn't considered when we think about teacher growth. Brooks and Brooks (1999) capture the learning relationship quite well: "When students work with adults who continue to view themselves as learners, who ask questions with which they themselves still grapple, who are willing and able to alter both content and practice in the pursuit of meaning, and who treat students and their endeavors as works in progress, not finished products, students are more likely to demonstrate these characteristics themselves" (p. 10).

An important aspect of *meaningful* is ensuring that the goals are appropriate for the teacher's experience. When a teacher is in his first year at New City School, for example, I assign the goal "to become familiar with New City School's philosophy, staff, and curriculum." This goal formalizes the awareness and learning through which any new teacher should proceed. The goal also allows me to periodically ask how the process is going and what has been learned. For someone who is in a new work setting, it is essential to learn the environment—the written and unwritten rules, as well as the personalities; having this as a formal goal makes the pursuit of this knowledge highly meaningful. (Sometimes, experienced teachers who are new to us tend to minimize what needs to be learned, and it can be difficult for them to accept this as a goal. Yet this goal is valid for all teachers who are new to us, regardless of their experience.)

Meaningful goals reflect not only a teacher's destination but her starting point as well. The goals of seasoned teachers should reflect their knowledge and skills and should be challenging. Without ever observing or even knowing the teachers on a

If you don't know where you are going, it makes no difference whether you are traveling by plane or by bicycle. ~Mahmoud faculty, we should be able to discern their relative skill and proficiency simply by reading their professional goals.

Goals Should Be Measurable

If you can't measure a goal, how can you determine whether you have succeeded? It's only logical that goals should be measurable. But what if your goal is "to increase student motivation" or "to generate excitement about learning"? Important and relevant as these goals might be, they do not readily lend themselves to a number. They're *measurable,* but not necessarily *quantifiable*. Thus, how goals are measured is a critical issue.

In measuring goals, it is appropriate to look at mean scores, average gains, and standard deviations. Traditional tests can play a role in documenting progress. However, not all goals need to be—or should be—quantifiable. As we look at both *what* students learn and *how* they learn, it is obvious that some goals do not lend themselves to quantification. Instead of backing away from these goals, we need to find new ways to monitor progress toward them.

Indeed, creativity is often needed to track some of the most important objectives. Consider monitoring the goal "to increase student motivation" or "to generate excitement about learning." Although tracking student attendance would yield quantifiable data, there are other, richer ways of capturing these attitudes. Student surveys and journal entries by students and teachers come to mind. Granted, surveys often *do* yield numerical data, but such numbers are quite different from test scores. Similarly, noting the degree to which students choose to pursue complex or difficult projects, or how eager they are to participate in class discussions, offers important information that could capture motivation or enthusiasm.

Rubric-based assessments and checklists also can be used to evaluate these kinds of attitudes and behaviors. Again, even though test data have their place, not all goals need to be measured this way. Some of the most important goals—those that

We have only one goal: to ignite the learning fire in all faculty members and our students. ~Pei Jen focus on students' attitudes and values—are best measured by valid but not readily quantifiable data. Finally, in thinking about goals that are measurable but not necessarily quantifiable, we should also embrace the idea that much good can come from teachers working creatively to determine how progress toward goals can be measured and recorded.

Goals Should Be Achievable

Teachers should feel that their goals are achievable, that with hard work and concentrated effort they can attain them. We must set realistic goals that are neither too easy nor too difficult. An advantage of setting multiple goals is that some goals can and should be challenging whereas others can and should be less so. A variety of goals is important.

Implicit in this statement is the belief that teachers should set more than one goal each year. The administration can help by promoting the expectation that teachers will *not* achieve every goal they set. If a teacher realizes all her goals, then the goals were not ambitious enough; if a teacher realizes none of her goals, then they were too arduous and unrealistic. The dialogue between teachers and principals about what constitutes a difficult goal and which goals are "almost a given" is, in itself, a productive exercise. (See *Stretch Goals* on p. 56 for more thoughts on this topic.)

Although setting more than one goal is helpful, we have to guard against the tendency, particularly by experienced, skilled teachers, to set too many goals. Years ago, one of my more talented and driven teachers came to her annual review with a list of her goals for the following year—all 16 of them! I gasped and responded that I appreciated her motivation and global view of our school, but 16 goals were simply too many to pursue effectively while staying relatively sane. After much debate, we narrowed her focus to five goals (though three would have been better!). This teacher still works with me, and each year at her review, we laugh about her 16 goals. However, each year she still brings in more goals than are reasonable, and we work together to help her focus. This negotiation has become an annual ritual for us.

Goals Should Be Individualized

Goals should reflect the interplay between the teaching context and a teacher's talents, and no two teachers or school contexts are the same. Further, even if two teachers of similar talent level were teaching comparable students at the same school, their goals might be identical, but the strategies to achieve these goals would be very different. In fact, often there is more variation in the strategies for how goals will be pursued than in the goals themselves. Just as we respect each student as a unique learner, we must respect each teacher. Developing different strategies for accomplishing their goals, including creating new assessment tools, is a great way for teachers to stay excited about their work and to keep growing. In situations in which the same goals are kept from year to year, experimenting with different strategies to achieve these goals is essential if teachers are to avoid becoming stagnant.

> It's important to have specific goals, but they need to be reflected upon. ~Bonnie

Sometimes, what appeals most to experienced and talented teachers is an opportunity to develop curriculum or to take on a leadership role with other adults. To the degree that they can become teachers of teachers within their schools, everyone gains. (Of course, sometimes these kinds of teachers are so skilled because they eschew much interaction with their peers and focus all their energies on their students. It is hard to complain about this dedication, and yet I am convinced that everyone benefits from a collegial setting.)

Kinds of Goals

The effectiveness of the goal-setting process—the degree to which it benefits both students and teachers—is rooted in the effectiveness of the goals themselves. As discussed, goals need to be meaningful, measurable, achievable, and individualized. In addition, there are different kinds of goals. Typically, the administrator chooses which kind of goal to pursue, though often with teacher input, depending upon the experience and talents of the teacher. The kind of goal that is chosen will frame the way a teacher thinks about the goal and the strategies for achieving it.

Stretch Goals

Although I noted earlier that goals must be achievable, stretch goals are a bit different. Stretch goals are so challenging, so global, or so ideal that a teacher cannot reasonably be expected to achieve them. "Then why set such a goal?" you may ask. Stretch goals are important because the efforts to achieve them can result in positive outcomes, whether or not the goals are achieved.

Great's worst enemy is good. ~Lynn

As a result of her years of excellent performance, a teacher should earn the right to have a stretch goal. An example of a stretch goal might be "to use no textbooks or worksheets in my teaching" or "to personally visit the parents of each of my students in their homes" or "to have each of my students achieve at the 95th percentile or better on our standardized tests."

The administrator usually raises the possibility of a stretch goal and offers it to the teacher. I cannot emphasize enough that stretch goals should not be set by all, or even by most, teachers. Being given the opportunity to set a stretch goal is a big compliment to the teacher. A stretch goal implies that the teacher is already extraordinarily proficient and that—and this is a separate issue—the teacher has the wisdom to appreciate the merit in setting a goal for which she is not likely to achieve success. That is, the teacher understands the rationale behind this strategy and accepts that the invitation to set a stretch goal is high praise from the administrator.

The words *offers, opportunity,* and *invitation* are important because a stretch goal should be voluntary. A potential problem is that teachers who are offered opportunities to set stretch goals are those who, by definition, are very hard workers with exceptionally high standards for themselves. They enjoy challenges. Unless setting a stretch goal is done carefully, however, these teachers can make themselves crazy by trying to achieve their stretch goals. Then they can become disappointed and upset when they are not successful.

Stretch goals are appropriate for administrators, too. My stretch goal for the past several years has been "to make/maintain New City School as a visible educational leader, both within and outside of the St. Louis community." I have pursued this primarily through our faculty's work with the theory of multiple intelligences and our efforts with collegiality. It is a good stretch goal because even though I will never fully accomplish it, the pursuit makes us a better school and helps me to grow. As a result of this stretch goal, I focus on the curriculum, teaching, and assessment techniques that will enable us to be a national leader in implementing multiple intelligences. I also focus on how collegiality can be used to help our faculty grow. Through my presentations at conferences and workshops, along with my writing, I also try to be a voice for multiple intelligences and faculty collegiality in communities outside St. Louis and around the world. I continually reflect on how our school can improve and what role I should be playing to facilitate everyone's growth, including my own. Pursuing my stretch goal yields many benefits to New City School and to me.

Goals work best for me when I generate them myself, rather than having a topic handed to me. ~Lucie

Team Goals

In addition to individual goals, there is much to be gained from teachers' working together to set team goals. Team goals are generated collaboratively by a team of teachers, and all team members are accountable for them. The teachers in a high school social studies department might develop a team goal to revise curriculum or to use student portfolios in assessment. A team of 4th grade teachers might decide on a team goal to involve their students in community service. Perhaps a team of teachers would make improving their communication with parents a priority or, even, set a team goal to work better together as colleagues. Think of the power in a dialogue about what a team's shared goal should be and how it should be measured and monitored! There is much collegial merit in having teams meet to share their goals and how they plan to measure them, as well as in periodically gathering to discuss the progress that has been made. Team goals are a good way to provide leadership opportunities to faculty veterans and to enable them to help younger teachers develop.

At New City School, we ask teaching teams to generate one team goal each year. The administration selects the area for the goal, and the team must determine its goal and how progress will be measured. Over the past few years, team goals have focused on capitalizing on our newly created New City School Centennial Garden, communicating better with students' parents, and developing math assessment tools to correspond to our new report cards. Another team goal falls under the category of recognizing the differences between consumers (students) and customers (their parents).

School Focus Goals

School focus goals are usually top-down goals that either are directly tied to a school theme (such as in a magnet school) or are a response to a schoolwide problem (such as low achievement or behavior issues). Whether the school's goal is to improve scores to a certain level on a particular test or to achieve a level of excellence in artistic or athletic performance, the focus can be so narrow that teachers are given little leeway in the goals that they develop or in the strategies that they wish to use. If this is the case, it is imperative that teachers also develop their own additional professional goals. (A school focus goal that would be an exception to this narrow approach would be to prepare for an accreditation visit or to implement a new curriculum.)

Mission-Based Goals

Mission-based goals may seem similar to school focus goals, but they are quite different. Mission-based goals are derived from a school's mission or philosophy. Although a school's philosophy and mission are periodically reviewed and revised, they are not likely to undergo significant change; these kinds of statements tend to be more global and less ephemeral. As a consequence, teachers who write goals derived from and supporting a school's philosophy or mission statement will typically be given great latitude in shaping these goals.

Consider the New City School mission statement:

> New City School is an urban school in which children from age 3 through 6th grade participate in a joyful and challenging education. In our creative environment, children become confident and knowledgeable about themselves and others. We prepare children to become successful, compassionate, and ethical learners through a combination of academics, ambience, and diversity.

My goals are simple: survive each day and enjoy as much as I can. ~Adrienne

From this mission statement, teachers might select goals in a variety of areas. They could develop materials or pedagogical practices to provide a joyful education, to provide a challenging education, to enable children to become confident and knowledgeable about themselves, to enable children to become confident and knowledgeable about others, or to enable children to become successful, compassionate, and ethical learners. Similarly, there are times when we have asked teachers to develop a goal that addresses one of our three major components: academics, ambience, and diversity.

One-Year and Multi-Year Goals

Significant and lasting progress doesn't happen in one year. Further, even if gains are made in one year, the next year is needed to solidify and review the gains. That means that most goals will require more than one year to be accomplished.

The fact that achieving a goal requires more than one year doesn't mean that progress isn't monitored and that the goal isn't reviewed and modified at the end of each year. For newer or less talented teachers, a shorter time frame might be appropriate. As a teacher gains expertise, it makes sense for him to take a longer view of his students' and his own development. Multi-year goals offer the advantage of helping us take the long view and avoid short-term solutions.

Private and Public Goals

At the start of this chapter, I mentioned the importance of sharing goals and working on them collaboratively. Not only does such dialogue enhance faculty collegiality, but teachers gain from the interaction and inspiration. However, private goals—those that are shared only between teacher and administrator—also have a place. These may be goals that address a teacher's shortcoming or area of need, where confidentiality is important. Or the goals might address something the teacher would not want shared broadly. Private goals may also focus on the dynamics of a teacher's team or leadership within the building, something that neither the teacher nor principal wants to talk about publicly.

For example, at New City School's end-of-year professional growth conferences (those times when teachers receive their year-end evaluations and contracts for the following year), almost every year a different teacher talks to me about difficulties that she has in interacting with another faculty member. (There are 45 people on my faculty, so this level of dissension is not as significant as it may sound!) In almost all cases, working to address the situation becomes a goal for the teacher. The teacher and I plan together and periodically meet to see what progress is being made, but this is not a public goal. Sometimes the concern gets translated into teacher leadership, and the teacher and I plan how she might play more of a leadership role within her teaching team or the faculty.

Sometimes, typically at my behest, the teacher with the concern subsequently shares her thoughts with the teacher who was

Life without goals is like a race with no finish line. ~Tamala confounding her. Occasionally the two teachers can work out their differences simply by talking about them and being more aware of their interactions. But sometimes this sharing results in the three of us meeting about how work relationships can be improved.

Often, when I meet with teammates who are having difficulties working as colleagues, I begin by asking each of them to write down three things that they enjoy about working with the other person and three things that drive them crazy. Before they share their lists, I ask them to also write what they speculate the other person has written. Doing this forces them to step back and try to see how they are perceived. I emphasize the word *perception* and remind them that perceptions are reality; we react to what we see and feel, whether or not it is the truth. That understanding helps move them away from denying their colleague's feelings and from focusing only on "what really happened" (which is what *they* think happened). Instead, as we share what they wrote, we work on seeing how we come across to others and what we can do to change impressions and perceptions. These meetings are never easy; it is difficult to see ourselves through the lenses of others. But such honest interactions are almost always productive.

Personal/Professional Goals

Distinct both from personal goals (learning how to play tennis or going to the gym three days a week) and from professional goals (learning about a new curriculum or how to use a new technology), personal/professional goals are those that focus on an individual's personality, leadership style, or balance in life, and how this affects work performance. Setting personal/professional goals helps teachers understand their roles as members of a learning community. Everyone benefits when the members of a faculty, including the administrators, look at the effect that their interactions can have on others.

Although most teacher goals should be professional ones, there are times when it is appropriate to set a professional goal

Another Explanation of Personal/Professional Goals

In September 2004, I began writing a bimonthly column for *Educational Leadership*, "The Principal Connection." My first article focused on the personal/professional goals described in this chapter, but with a twist on how to generate and monitor them.

What is your goal for the year? I'm not talking about a goal assigned to you or imposed by No Child Left Behind. I'm asking about the goal you have chosen for yourself.

Although you wouldn't know it from my infrequent workouts at the gym, I believe we all need to set goals and work toward achieving them. Goals give us focus, and our progress in meeting them provides us with instant feedback. Without focusing our efforts, we are less likely to succeed. Indeed, without goals, how can we know whether or not we have succeeded?

Educators' goals are typically tied to student success. We want a greater percentage of students to pass; we want to improve student attendance; we want students doing better in X, Y, or Z (or, more likely, in X, Y, *and* Z). Sometimes our goals are professionally oriented: We want to improve this pedagogical technique, we want to develop that curriculum, or we want to create a new professional development plan. It's hard to argue with these kinds of goals.

But as important as professional goals are, they don't address who we are as people. Goals that focus only on student progress, pedagogy, and curriculum ignore the way we function and grow and the way we work with and lead others. Yet these factors are crucial to our success and to the success of those we work with.

We need to set *personal/professional goals*. These are different from purely personal goals (losing weight or learning how to play the piano) and different from purely professional goals (writing curriculum or raising test scores). Personal/professional goals focus on the effect that such factors as personality, leadership style, and balance have on our performance at work.

But how do you decide on a goal? I went through a *360 evaluation*, a performance assessment based entirely on the perceptions of the 30-plus people who work with me. It was both affirming and humbling. The process forced me to come to grips with who I am as a person

that focuses on a personal, nonschool issue. For this to happen, the comfort and trust level between the teacher and administrator needs to be strong. In most cases, the genesis for this kind of goal comes from the teacher. The issue might relate to reducing personal stress, or dealing with a health concern, or maybe and how that affects who I am as a professional. I learned, for example, that at times I seem too goal-oriented and focused and that I need to do a better job of listening to others. (*What?*) As a result, I set personal/professional goals to address these areas.

Not everyone has to set a goal this way. During an inservice session this August, I talked with faculty members about setting their own goals. I explained that although these goals would remain private, they had to relate to teachers' effectiveness at work. At our next faculty meeting, each teacher wrote his or her goal on a piece of paper and sealed it in an envelope labeled with his or her name. We then placed all our envelopes in a box (mine included) and ceremoniously taped it shut. After we finished, I announced that in May—just before the teachers' end-of-year professional growth conferences—I would return their unopened envelopes to them. At each teacher's final conference, I would ask whether or not the teacher had succeeded in attaining his or her goal, and whether I could help him or her reach it in any way. I also emphasized that sharing any information about the goal would be entirely up to the teacher.

Setting the goal is only the first step, of course, and monitoring teachers' progress on achieving their private goals will not be easy. Nevertheless, throughout the year I plan to periodically remind faculty members about their personal/professional goals, asking such questions as, "How do you think you're doing on your goal?" and "If someone knew your goal, what might he or she say about your progress?" Supporting teachers' progress in achieving their personal/professional goals fosters a climate of collaboration and collegiality. As a result, everyone in the building benefits.

Not every goal will be achieved; I know that. But I also know that the goal-setting process alone is beneficial. We all gain when we stop to reflect on our interactions with others and consider the influence those interactions have on our performance. In a future column, I'll share some of what I heard from my teachers as they reflected on their progress, and I'll also share a bit about how well I achieved my own personal/professional goals. Now it's time for you to set your own goal—where's that envelope? (Hoerr, 2004, pp. 86–87)

balancing home and school or adjusting to a new spouse or child. Or perhaps the teacher's goal is to become a school administrator.

In these personal, more private growth scenarios, the term *goal* implies more formality than is the case. In my experience, putting these issues on the table is a healthy step. But unlike with professional goals, the strategies to accomplish personal goals are often vaguer and far less measurable. That said, because these issues are important, growth still is a priority. One way to increase the chance for success is to be diligent about meeting periodically to monitor progress.

Of course, personal issues that affect our professional roles are common, almost pervasive. This is true regardless of a teacher's experience, knowledge, or skill level. Simply because a teacher performs at an excellent level day in and day out, we should not assume that personal issues are not a factor in her performance. Indeed, sometimes the focus, drive, and commitment that are needed to attain this status come with a personal cost. Administrators who fail to recognize how a teacher's personal life can influence her professional life are naive, if not foolish.

One way that we have tried to address the relationship between personal and professional lives at New City School is through our mentor process. All first- and second-year teachers have mentors, other teachers with whom they regularly meet, and they also meet monthly with an administrator. In recognition of the importance of personal issues, half of these monthly meetings are led by our school counselor. At these sessions, where neither I nor another administrator is present, our new teachers are free to bring up issues from home that they carry to the workplace. Our school counselor hears their concerns and offers them assistance or refers them to some other place. Because of the counselor's training, the teachers are comfortable in bringing personal issues to her. (Sometimes, of course, they do this sharing privately, one-on-one.)

Goals for Administrators

Administrators should have goals, too. We certainly don't want to be wandering along with Alice! The characteristics and kinds

> The problem with goals is that they sometimes make teachers (and learners) feel like targets. ~Brian

of goals described here for teachers apply equally well to administrators. In addition to setting goals and sharing them with their supervisors, however, administrators should share some, not necessarily all, of their goals with the faculty. Doing this models the goal-setting process. That is, it vividly demonstrates to teachers that goals should be meaningful, measurable, achievable, and individualized. It is also an opportunity for an administrator to show that the progress toward attaining a goal is never straight and smooth and requires both focus and tenacity.

Sometimes it is important for teachers to be reminded that they and their administrators are operating under much the same pressure and constraints. When an administrator shares a goal with her faculty and asks for input, it shouts that everyone is on the same team. This can be the start of a wonderfully collaborative dialogue and should increase the probability of the goal being achieved.

It can be tempting to form goals that only reflect our school and our faculty. That is hard to argue with; after all, our schools are our jobs. But it's also good for administrators to set professional goals that focus on their skill set or knowledge. Whether it's learning how to use a new piece of technology, gaining an understanding of the school budget, or pursuing a new model of teacher evaluation, administrators need to consciously work at learning and keeping themselves current.

Last year, for example, one of my goals was to learn how to use PowerPoint. *How hard can this be*, I thought. *Our 4th graders learn this skill!* Well, old dogs can learn new tricks, and I have mastered (OK, semi-mastered) PowerPoint. I really didn't have the time to do this, though, and it wasn't always easy. If I hadn't publicly announced this goal, it's likely that I would have put it on the back burner and never learned the skill. Today, I'm very glad I took the time and forced myself to learn PowerPoint. I routinely use it at meetings and wonder why I waited so long to learn it.

I like that we had a personal/professional goal this year that we could keep private. Sometimes it feels forced to make a goal fit in a box, especially when you really want to work on something else. ~April

The Power of Goals

The monitoring of goals needs as much attention as goal setting. All too often, a great deal of energy is placed on establishing goals, and far less attention is given to how progress toward them can be monitored. Once goal setting is completed, the pace of the school year overwhelms us, and we don't give sufficient attention to what progress is being made and what modifications should be made in our strategies. Opportunities for student and teacher learning are lost when goals are set in the fall and ignored until spring. The best way to avoid this trap is to schedule periodic times throughout the school year when individuals will touch base and share their progress. Scheduled in the fall when the goals are developed, these interactions could be formal, one-on-one meetings between a teacher and an administrator, or they could be small-group conversations among teachers at faculty meetings or through e-mail exchanges.

Teachers feel like many goals are revisited too frequently and are based on the visions of others. ~Tarren

At my school, we sometimes designate faculty meetings for updates on goal progress. Teachers are also placed into discussion groups based on the similarity of their goals, and these groups meet a few times during the year. The small settings and common focus allow teachers to share their progress and learn from what others are doing to address similar issues. At least one face-to-face meeting between teachers and administrators that is focused on teacher goals must take place each year. After all, if administrators don't take the time to talk to teachers about goals, what is the message we give about their importance?

Teachers' goals should be an important tool in their professional development and in moving a school forward. Goals can focus efforts and help teachers balance their lives; they can be used to address teacher shortcomings and extend teacher strengths; they can be used to facilitate teamwork and to achieve schoolwide goals. For this to happen, though, the goal-setting process needs to be a priority of the principal. Her involvement will vary, depending upon the needs of the school, characteristics of the teacher, and type of goal. However, it must be clear to everyone that setting and attaining goals is important. This importance can be made obvious by the attention given to the formulation of goals and the monitoring of their progress.

5 Wielding Power

Too often, backs stiffen and eyebrows rise when the word *power* is used in an organizational context. As a culture, we are often wary of power; as a profession, we are usually uncomfortable with power. What this really means is that we are uncomfortable with other people having power over us. For better or worse (actually, for better *and* worse), education attracts people who don't seek a great deal of power and who tend to hold an egalitarian world view. As a result, we may have difficulty seeing that there is nothing inherently negative about power; what matters is how power is used.

Power is the ability to produce an effect; it is control, influence, and authority over others. Simply put, power is the ability to cause others to do what you want them to do. Yet there is nothing simple about getting and using power. As noted in Chapter 3, attitudes about power have changed. Today, the power that administrators need cannot be given to them; they must earn their power.

If administrators lack power or fail to use the power that they have (which is the same as not having the power in the first place), chaos ensues. Sometimes the chaos is loud, with disagreements, destructive battles, a lack of clarity about the organization's direction, or outright rebellion. At other times the chaos is quiet, characterized by a high degree of apathy, with each person following his or her own path, moving toward and arriving at a range of destinations. In either case, if the person running the school lacks power, it bodes poorly for everyone, including the students. Of course, power that is used negatively bodes poorly as well. How power is used is a significant factor in a school's culture and in determining whether or not that school attracts and supports strong teachers.

Before discussing forms of power and how school leaders might cultivate them, take time to reflect on the kinds of professional power that *you* currently have. Please complete the power inventory presented in Figure 3 on p. 70. The implications of your responses will be discussed at the end of the chapter.

Five Kinds of Power

The classic model of social power, set out by French and Raven (1959), identifies five different sources of power: reward, coercive, legitimate, referent, and expert. Each of these stems from a different power base. Whenever people do what we have asked or acquiesce to our demands, they are doing so in response to our having one or more of these power bases.

Leaders provide as much positive support as possible. ~Barry

Typically, leaders possess more than one type of power and use these powers in combination with one another. None of us can ever possess all five kinds of power in any situation or with any individual, but an awareness of the power bases is helpful as we think about how to supervise teachers and move a school forward.

Reward Power

Reward power is based on an individual's ability to give rewards to others. The rewards can be tangible or intangible. Although we may tend to think of rewards as tangible, intangible rewards are often the most important. When you tell a teacher that her lesson was superb (and recount exactly what made it superb), you are not just complimenting her. You are using reward power, which reinforces her past actions and influences her future behaviors. Asking a teacher if she would like to head a committee, take responsibility for making a presentation at a

Figure 3

A Power Inventory

Identify three individuals who follow your professional lead, whether or not you officially supervise them. Use their initials to indicate their identity:

Person A _____   Person B _____   Person C _____

Check off those statements that explain why each individual responds to your direction.

Person A follows my lead because he or she . . .

1. Recognizes that I am the boss . . . . ❑
2. Holds me in high esteem . . . . ❑
3. Understands that I am knowledgeable . . . ❑
4. Does anything to avoid negative feedback . . . . . ❑
5. Realizes that I have the ability to reward him or her . . . . ❑
6. Doesn't want to be criticized . . . . ❑
7. Defers to my hierarchical position . . . ❑
8. Knows I have skills and understandings . . . ❑
9. Accepts that this is his or her role . . . . ❑
10. Thrives on positive feedback from me . . . . . ❑
11. Wants to be like me . . . . ❑
12. Views me as a role model . . . . ❑
13. Lives for praise . . . . . . ❑
14. Is worried about job security . . . . ❑
15. Defers to my expertise . . ❑

Person B follows my lead because he or she . . .

1. Recognizes that I am the boss . . . . ❑
2. Holds me in high esteem . . . . ❑
3. Understands that I am knowledgeable . . . ❑
4. Does anything to avoid negative feedback . . . . . ❑
5. Realizes that I have the ability to reward him or her . . . . ❑
6. Doesn't want to be criticized . . . . ❑
7. Defers to my hierarchical position . . . ❑
8. Knows I have skills and understandings . . . ❑
9. Accepts that this is his or her role . . . . ❑
10. Thrives on positive feedback from me . . . . . ❑
11. Wants to be like me . . . . ❑
12. Views me as a role model . . . . ❑
13. Lives for praise . . . . . . ❑
14. Is worried about job security . . . . ❑
15. Defers to my expertise . . ❑

Person C follows my lead because he or she . . .

1. Recognizes that I am the boss . . . . ❑
2. Holds me in high esteem . . . . ❑
3. Understands that I am knowledgeable . . . ❑
4. Does anything to avoid negative feedback . . . . . ❑
5. Realizes that I have the ability to reward him or her . . . . ❑
6. Doesn't want to be criticized . . . . ❑
7. Defers to my hierarchical position . . . ❑
8. Knows I have skills and understandings . . . ❑
9. Accepts that this is his or her role . . . . ❑
10. Thrives on positive feedback from me . . . . . ❑
11. Wants to be like me . . . . ❑
12. Views me as a role model . . . . ❑
13. Lives for praise . . . . . . ❑
14. Is worried about job security . . . . ❑
15. Defers to my expertise . . ❑

parent assembly, or supervise a student teacher is also using reward power. Each of these roles signifies a vote of confidence and is a reward for performance. (However, these examples work as rewards *only* when the teacher views them as rewards. Some teachers might think that these responsibilities are a burden. A good administrator will know her teachers well enough to anticipate correctly what they perceive as a reward.)

Rewards can be mundane or minor and still be effective. Years ago, we gave each of our teachers a desktop computer and a school e-mail account. I wanted to move us from paper to electronic communications, and I began sending e-mail messages instead of putting handwritten or typed notes in teachers' mailboxes. Much to my dismay, moving to electronic correspondence was harder than I anticipated. Getting teachers into the habit of regularly checking their computers for an e-mail message was no easy task. My requests to check e-mail were met with eye-rolling and groans. Clearly, "drastic" measures were necessary.

Candy never lasts long in the teachers' lounge, so I purchased $30 worth of candy bars, put them in a huge bag, and took them to a faculty meeting. Everyone's eyes were on me as I dangled the bag in the air. "In an effort to get you to check regularly for e-mail messages," I began, "I will be offering candy bars as prizes. Periodically during the day, I will send an e-mail to everyone on the faculty, and a candy bar will go to the fifth person who responds to me." (I rewarded the fifth rather than the first person so that there would be no incentive to sit by the computer and respond immediately.) Within days, the situation changed dramatically. For example, I sent this e-mail message: "Who wants a chocolate bar with nuts? The fifth person who responds will be the winner. And, by the way, because the temperature is below 20 degrees, there will be no outside recess." I received response after response from my teachers, logging in to win the candy. Best of all, no teachers lined up their classes to take them outside to recess. After a week or so—and lots of candy bars!—I no longer needed to offer a reward because the

I feel terrified when I hear that an inspector is coming to evaluate me. I wish I could be swallowed by the ground. ~Mahmoud teachers were in the habit of checking for e-mail several times each day.

On a far more serious level, I recently became aware of a conference on diversity that was being held in Hawaii. I told the teachers on our Diversity Committee that if two or three of them submitted a proposal to present at the conference and it was accepted, we would pay their way to attend. Sure enough, a group of three submitted a proposal, and it was accepted. Although getting to Hawaii from St. Louis is not cheap, this opportunity was a clear reward for their efforts. (As well, this expenditure was a statement to our teachers about the value we place on diversity and on the importance of their professional growth.) Similarly, a techno-savvy teacher who has taken the lead in finding ways to use technology to help students learn was rewarded by having his classroom chosen to pilot a SMART Board. (A SMART Board is a touch-sensitive computerized whiteboard from which you can digitally capture writing, manipulate projected images, navigate the Internet, and direct any of the other normal controls from a computer.) The teacher had expressed a great deal of interest in obtaining this tool, and I authorized the purchase to reinforce his enthusiasm for finding ways to use technology in the classroom.

Not all rewards cost money; indeed, most do not. Perhaps the best reward—again, depending upon how this is viewed by the teacher—is providing an opportunity to shine in front of others. Inviting a teacher to present to peers at faculty or committee meetings can be a wonderful way to offer kudos. One spring, I was concerned about the negative interactions among our students because they weren't living our school philosophy of respecting one another. A faculty committee was formed to look at this issue and make recommendations. I asked a teacher who was new to us to chair the group. This invitation was a very salient way of rewarding her for her skills and energy. Similarly, I have had teachers who were particularly creative in using multiple intelligences (MI) theory share their successes at faculty

> A good leader knows when to get involved and when to let the experts do their work.
>
> ~Sue

meetings. Doing this not only helped others use MI; it also was a way of rewarding those who had taken the initiative. A teacher could also be offered a chance to make a presentation at a parent meeting or to the board of directors. The positive feedback that teachers receive from these sorts of presentations provides strong reward power.

Occasionally, teachers have the opportunity to make presentations to outsiders. At New City School, for example, hundreds of educators visit us each year to learn about our work in implementing MI theory, and sometimes we give a formal presentation before they tour our school and visit classrooms. Our more experienced teachers often meet with these groups, but on a number of occasions I have asked teachers in their second or third year at New City School if they would like to be part of the formal presentation. They usually see this opportunity as a reward.

All forms of power, especially reward power, are subjective. A reward is only a reward if it is perceived that way by the person being rewarded. Some teachers would dread the presentation opportunities that I have described (and for them, making a presentation would be an example of *coercive* power!). Developing reward power begins with a principal's knowing her teachers and understanding what motivates them. This knowledge has many benefits, as Murphy (2002) observes: "Those people who feel that they are truly understood may be more likely to listen to the leader's ideas and implement his or her plans" (p. 174).

Coercive Power

Coercive power is the reciprocal of reward power. It is the power we have due to our ability to punish (or to remove a reward, which has the same effect). Coercive power often isn't talked about in polite circles. We are a bit uncomfortable in acknowledging that we possess coercive power, and we don't like to think of ourselves playing a coercive role. But a good leader must have the ability to use both the carrot and the stick, to reward and to punish. Obviously, absolutely, and certainly, the carrot is far preferable to the stick, yet there are situations in which it is necessary to use coercive power. Always, this must be done with delicacy and with respect.

Just as power makes some uncomfortable, the thought that an administrator would have, much less use, *coercive* power raises the blood pressure of many. Reality, however, tells us that good administrators use coercive power. They use it well, and they use it rarely, but they do use it.

I've been leading schools for 28 years. Hard discussions with staff members—discussions in which I have to use my coercive power—are no easier for me today than they were when I began. But the ability to initiate the hard conversation and let a teacher know that you are disappointed in his performance is one of the qualities that sets apart good administrators. A principal has an obligation to talk to the teacher who continues to make the same old mistake, time after time. A cause-and-effect relationship needs to be established. The teacher, even if he is a star teacher (especially if he is a star teacher), needs to understand that his actions have consequences. When the relationship with the teacher is based on trust and respect, the principal's unhappiness or disappointment becomes a kind of punishment. Yet the goal is to help the teacher reflect on and change behavior, not to punish. Because the teacher values the principal's opinion, the criticism and disappointment will carry a sting. Teachers need to know that their performance is important and that their actions will elicit appropriate rewards and punishments.

The key here is *appropriate*. Principals must ensure that their reactions, whether positive or negative (but especially when they are negative), fit the situation. We must work to be sure that we respond to an incident based only on the incident, not on what has been happening for the past one hour, two days, three weeks, or four months. When I'm upset, I've learned to take a deep breath and sit on the issue for a couple of hours or an evening. I'm often amazed at how much less significant many things seem a day later. (And if something is equally significant a day later, then it probably really is significant!)

There is power when everyone knows the penalties for poor performance. The strongest teachers gain from the awareness that both reward and coercive measures exist, even though their level of proficiency means that they may never experience the coercive side. However, when a teacher sees someone else being chastised for a poor performance, it makes the positives that she has been given even more meaningful. (Even though criticisms should always be done in private, the word often seeps out.)

Years ago, for example, there was a teacher at New City School who occasionally was dyspeptic with her students. Although I rarely saw evidence of this, another teacher would express dissatisfaction to me about her. Sometimes I would hear about her moods from her students' parents. The teacher and I talked about this issue a few times, but she always denied that there was a problem. Nevertheless, I felt the need to address this topic in her year-end professional growth conference.

Our contract process dictated that each teacher meet with me and receive an evaluation for the present year and a contract for the next one. (This is still true today.) The meetings were held in the conference room, just across the hall from the teachers' lounge. This particular teacher and I met during lunch to review her evaluation, which she had received the previous day. The document noted my concern about her being grumpy and short with her students. No sooner had I welcomed her to the meeting than she slammed her evaluation sheet on the table. Her face turned red, and her eyes widened. Before I could say anything, she yelled, almost at the top of her lungs, "Negative about students? You think I'm too negative with my students? You think I'm too critical? Well, you're wrong, and I'm tired of being criticized for this!"

With that, she opened the door to the conference room and stomped out, slamming it loudly behind her. She passed by the open door to the teachers' lounge as she returned to her

> The best leaders are those who never ask you to do something they would not do or to give more than they would give. ~Sheryl

classroom. The lounge was as quiet as a tomb because the teachers who were there eating lunch had heard her voice, heard the door slam, and seen her leave. I sat there, stunned.

A few days later, in a follow-up meeting, she shared that on that particular morning, she and her husband had had a difficult confrontation at the breakfast table. Her tenuous temperament clearly wasn't helped by that interaction. What's relevant here, though, is that her yelling, slamming the door, and storming out of the room were heard and seen by everyone in the teachers' lounge. Further, it didn't take long for those teachers who weren't in the lounge to hear about what had happened.

Although none of us likes to see someone unhappy or in pain (this is especially true for teachers), the fact that most of the faculty witnessed or were aware of this incident gave more meaning to the positives that were written about them in their evaluations. Because they knew that poor performance was negatively rewarded, the positive narratives in their evaluations meant more. The reward power was increased. (The end of the story is that the teacher taught one more year at New City School and then "elected" to take a job elsewhere. Her decision to leave was due in part to the realization that if she remained with us, she was going to have to work to improve her temperament. I made it a priority at her goal-setting conference the following fall, and it was a topic at each subsequent meeting.)

Such interactions are never easy, and principals need to make sure that their negative reactions and use of coercive power fit the individual and situation. We expect our teachers to know and understand the differences among their students, so we must also know and understand the differences among the teachers themselves. Which teacher responds best to a mild chide? Who needs to be told something time and again for it to sink in? Who needs feedback or suggestions in writing? Which teachers require public praise, and who should never be singled out in any way? Recognizing individual differences and yet being consistent with everyone is an ongoing challenge. The lesson

> I follow leaders who evidence integrity, sincerity, compassion, and respect for others; who are visionary and optimistic; and who are anchors in storms. I want an administrator who looks out for the good of the whole rather than for the short, immediate interests of a few.
>
> ~Becky

that fair does not mean equal can be a hard one for adults (and children) to learn. Like many other important lessons, it is easiest to learn when it is put on the table and talked about directly. My experience is that most teachers are willing to understand that not every adult is treated the same when they see that how I interact with them, personally, takes their particular needs into consideration.

Legitimate Power

Legitimate power is determined by an individual's title and position. A person holds legitimate power solely by virtue of his or her hierarchical position. When we talk about individuals having the authority to perform a task, it usually means that they have power because of a formal role in the hierarchy. In essence, this form of power manifests itself in a "do it because I am your boss and I said so" attitude. Barth (2004) refers to this kind of influence as "positional power" (p. 106).

Legitimate power is the weakest power in today's questioning times. In many contexts, we no longer assume that those who are in charge know more than we do or should automatically be followed. Legitimate power alone won't allow you to accomplish much. Bolman and Deal (1997) note this reality: "Rarely will people provide their best efforts and fullest cooperation because they have been told to do so. They need to perceive the people in authority as credible, competent, and pursuing sensible directions" (p. 184).

The vitiation of legitimate power is not all bad. In the past, legitimate power was defined more broadly. Some would attribute legitimate power to others based on their gender, age, or race. For example, the assumption was that a fatigued Rosa Parks would stand on the bus simply because whites had legitimate power over blacks and deserved priority for seating. Fortunately, progress has been made in this area. Although our culture is far from perfect, more and more we judge people by the skills and talents they have, not by their race, gender, or the position they occupy. (When access to a position is based on skill or talent, such as with a physician or attorney, the deference that we offer is based not on their position, alone, but on the expertise they must possess to occupy it.)

Referent Power

Referent power is power that an individual has because others esteem her and identify with her. As a result of this admiration, they will do what she asks. Referent power stems from an individual's charisma. The individual who is charismatic often has others following her and doing her bidding simply because they like her and want to emulate her. This kind of power is largely personality based. Referent power is closely related to reward power and is the most difficult power to acquire.

A ringleader, whether leading a youth gang to engage in destructive behaviors or to volunteer time after school, probably influences his peers through his referent power. Presidents Ronald Reagan and Bill Clinton represent the opposite ends of the political spectrum, but from all accounts, they share an abundance of referent power. Conversely, Presidents Jimmy Carter and George H. W. Bush clearly lacked referent power. Referent power receives less attention in this book because of all of the forms of social power, it is the one we are least able to develop. Derived from charisma and personality, referent power is the least amenable to modification.

Expert Power

Expert power is based in one's knowledge or expertise. When our physician says, "Take this medicine twice each day, even though it may upset your stomach," we willingly submit ourselves to the discomfort because we trust her. Similarly, when the auto mechanic tells me that repairing my car will cost $188 because the thingamajig is broken, I pay without understanding what exactly is broken because he is the expert. He knows how the motor works, and I don't. In the same fashion, when our students' parents follow the recommendations that we make about their children, they are responding to our expert power.

This power transcends hierarchy and role. When a teacher willingly changes her behavior based on another's suggestion, she does so because she respects the wisdom—the expertise—of that colleague. In effect, the teacher is responding to her colleague's expert power (even though the colleague may not even know she possesses it). Teachers who follow a principal's lead because they respect her knowledge and know that she has analyzed the situation correctly are responding to her expert power. Expert power doesn't automatically come with her role; it is given to her by others based on her skills, knowledge, and expertise.

Development of Expert Power

Expert power is the most important power for school leaders and the one that they can most easily develop. If we are willing to show that we are knowledgeable, not by our edicts but by demonstrating what we know, we can earn the trust of our teachers, and they will give us expert power. We will not gain expert power just because of our scholastic degrees, experience, or title but because our teachers know that we have information, insights, and expertise that can help them do a better job. Our opportunities to demonstrate expert power come from our classroom observations, both formal and informal; from our participation in committee and ad hoc meetings; from our conferences with teachers; and from the way we lead meetings. We *earn* expert power by observing teachers and interacting with them: talking, questioning, reinforcing, supporting, prodding, and leading.

The principal's expertise comes through loudly and clearly when she visits a classroom and goes beyond lofty compliments to offer specific feedback and suggestions. Teachers will give the principal expert power when she raises thoughts about wait-time

If I know that someone cares about me and respects me and is open and truthful with me, then I will trust him and be faithful to him forever. ~Lucie and questioning techniques, or when she asks how a lesson was differentiated to address the range of student abilities. What a principal chooses to discuss says volumes about her expertise. A principal who visits classrooms and never speaks to the pedagogy is basically saying that she doesn't have much knowledge of or interest in teaching. A principal who talks only about student discipline or paperwork deadlines is really saying that curriculum and pedagogy are outside her area of expertise. When this happens, we cannot expect teachers to attribute any expert power to us or to follow any lead we may offer based on our knowledge.

Expert power is not necessarily derived from the fact that the principal has greater knowledge or expertise in a subject area or pedagogy. At the secondary school level, many faculty members have disciplinary knowledge that far exceeds what the principal knows; at the elementary school level, many teachers have knowledge of pedagogy and curriculum that far exceeds what the principal knows. (It is a fortunate principal who has well trained and highly knowledgeable teachers on her faculty!) Instead, the principal's expert power stems from knowing what questions to ask and from an ability and willingness to engage in a dialogue with a teacher that helps the teacher clarify his thinking and move forward.

Sometimes asking the right questions shows expertise as much as providing the correct answers does. To the degree that I have expert power, that is certainly true for me. I was a good teacher, yet I am surrounded by many teachers at New City School who are far better than I ever hoped to be. But that realization doesn't limit my ability to bring expert power to the situation and help them grow. Consider the discussion below between a star teacher, Helen, and her principal:

> I will follow a leader who knows what he is talking about and who can walk the walk.
>
> ~Debbie

Principal: How did you feel about that lesson?

Helen: I was pleased that the students seemed to understand my main points, how the geography and history of the North and South led the people living in

	these regions to have such different views of slavery.
Principal:	Do you think that all the students understood this? I could see Jose and Renee and Alicia nodding and responding well, but what about Cathy and Maurice in the back of the room?
Helen:	That is a good question. I guess I'll find out when I grade their tests on Friday.
Principal:	Is there any way you could have structured the lesson or asked your questions differently so that you could have known this during the lesson?

At this point, the principal is only asking and has not offered any knowledge or proposed any solutions. Yet the principal's questions have demonstrated not just her interest but also her expertise. Principals who do possess subject-matter or pedagogical expertise can go beyond questioning and offer suggestions that help teachers. This support becomes more obvious as the principal continues:

Principal:	What if you had stopped about halfway through the lesson and asked the students to write on a piece of paper, in big letters, *North* and *South,* followed by something unique about each area's geography and history. You could have walked the perimeter of the room and gained a quick sense of who was on target and who was not. Or maybe you could have asked them to form small groups of three or four and assigned some groups history and others geography. Then they could have talked for a few minutes about how the North and South differed. Again, you could have eavesdropped on each of the groups or made a point of listening to the ones in which Cathy and Maurice were talking.

A principal can ask the following questions at a more general level, applicable to almost any lesson, to lead a teacher to think in a way that is beneficial to reflection and planning. These questions also allow the principal to demonstrate her expertise during the dialogue that will follow.

• How was this lesson different from the last time you taught it?

• What will you do differently the next time that you teach this lesson?

• How are you accommodating for your top students and your struggling students?

• What are you doing for the students in the middle, those whose performance places them neither at the top nor at the bottom of the classroom array?

• How might changing the way you assess students influence how you teach?

• How might changing the way you assess students influence who learns what?

• What do you learn if you look at students' performances by their race, gender, or socioeconomic status?

The most important quality for a leader is empathy. ~Mary Ann

Each of these questions is open ended and likely to elicit a rich exchange between the teacher and the principal. By engaging in this kind of discussion, the principal shows her interest and expertise. Both the principal and the teacher will learn from these dialogues. Invariably, the principal's expert power will increase from what she has learned from such interactions.

School leaders can do other things to show the faculty that they are more than paper-pushers or disciplinarians and, in fact, do possess some expert power. Personally, I read a lot and frequently distribute relevant articles or chapters to my faculty with an invitation to read the material. Sharing this way makes it easier to enter a discussion on a particular topic. Sharing books and articles also lets my teachers know that I am curious and pursue knowledge. Being an active faculty committee member is another way for a principal to gain and show expertise. Teachers, especially the strongest ones, don't expect their principals to know more than they do (and would often be surprised if this were the case), but they do expect and want their principals to be interested in their classrooms, their pedagogy, and their curriculum. Learning *with* teachers is a powerful way to gain and exhibit expert power.

Implications of the Power Inventory

At the beginning of this chapter, you were asked to complete an inventory that considered why others follow your lead (Figure 3 on p. 70). The items on the survey relate to the different power bases in the French and Raven (1959) model:

> • Items 5, 10, and 13 indicate that an individual follows due to your reward power.
>> • Items 4, 6, and 14 relate to your coercive power.
>> • Items 1, 7, and 9 stem from your legitimate power.
>> • Items 2, 11, and 12 address your referent power.
>> • Items 3, 8, and 15 indicate leadership due to your expert power.

The perfect balance of strength and gentleness is required.

~Sarah

Use Figure 4 on p. 84 to find out your score for each power base, combining your totals for Person A, Person B, and Person C. Each check mark is worth one point.

You may have a score of 9 in each of the five power bases (but not likely!). A score of 6 or higher in a power base indicates an area of strength for you. A score of 3 or less suggests an area of weakness. You can also gain insight about your power bases by considering the differences among scores—which forms of power are stronger or weaker—and reflecting on how your power varies by the individuals being influenced and led. In analyzing your scores, consider the following questions:

> • In which area or areas of power do you seem to be strongest?
> • Excluding referent power, because it is so personality driven, which kinds of power do you rarely use?

Figure 4

Power Inventory Scoring Chart

Reward power

Person A	Items 5 + 10 + 13	=	_____
Person B	Items 5 + 10 + 13	=	_____
Person C	Items 5 + 10 + 13	=	_____
	Reward total	=	_____

Coercive power

Person A	Items 4 + 6 + 14	=	_____
Person B	Items 4 + 6 + 14	=	_____
Person C	Items 4 + 6 + 14	=	_____
	Coercive total	=	_____

Legitimate power

Person A	Items 1 + 7 + 9	=	_____
Person B	Items 1 + 7 + 9	=	_____
Person C	Items 1 + 7 + 9	=	_____
	Legitimate total	=	_____

Referent power

Person A	Items 2 + 11 + 12	=	_____
Person B	Items 2 + 11 + 12	=	_____
Person C	Items 2 + 11 + 12	=	_____
	Referent total	=	_____

Expert power

Person A	Items 3 + 8 + 15	=	_____
Person B	Items 3 + 8 + 15	=	_____
Person C	Items 3 + 8 + 15	=	_____
	Expert total	=	_____

• Are the three individuals primarily responding to the same bases of power, or are there differences in the power base that are more effective?

• Thinking beyond these three individuals, does the power that you use change by the position and role of the people with whom you are working?

• Is there a difference in the proportion of your power bases now versus a decade ago?

Because our power is based on the perceptions of others, it is never static. Power is constantly changing, either increasing or decreasing. Effective school leaders are aware of their power profiles and work to ensure that they have the power to lead.

The Power of Perception

When teachers follow the leadership of a principal, their actions are a response to the combination of her forms of power: reward, coercive, legitimate, referent, and, most important, expert. This combination of powers and their effectiveness vary, of course, due to the characteristics and attitudes of the principal as well as the characteristics and attitudes of the teachers she is supervising.

> I appreciate a leader who is working as hard as or harder than I am, and that is obvious by his or her organizational skills.
> ~Tarren

We need to recognize that all power is based on the perceptions of others, in this case, those we are supervising. Barth (1980) expresses it this way: "Leadership is in the eyes of the led" (p. 184). That is, someone else can have power over us or we can have power over that person only to the degree that we agree, consciously or subconsciously, to enter into that relationship. If money or praise is not important to us, for example, it is not likely that others will have reward power over us. If we have no respect for someone, he will have no referent power over us. If someone is not our boss, she may have no legitimate power over us. And if others fail to recognize our knowledge or skill, we will have no expert power over them.

With that caveat in mind, we need to understand how school leaders can work to increase their power bases. Increasing your power bases begins with recognizing the perceptual nature of power and knowing the people you are supervising. Successful administrators understand those whom they supervise and recognize how they are perceived. With that knowledge, principals can develop an array of rewards that motivate and coercive measures that send a message. Most important, principals can actively begin to put themselves in situations in which they are learning and in which their teachers see them as learners. In schools, expert power is the strongest, and it is incumbent upon every principal to work to develop this area. For principals, power is used to influence others to increase student learning. Developing and wielding expert power has the greatest potential for bringing about the growth of faculty and staff members.

Evaluating
Teacher Growth

6

Evaluating teachers is one of the most important tasks that principals perform. Indeed, teacher evaluation may be *the* most important task. After all, what matters more to the quality of a school than the quality of its teachers? Neither the beauty and functionality of a school building nor the quality and relevance of a curriculum can begin to compare to the effect that an inspirational and skilled teacher has on students.

When adults talk about their educational experiences and reflect on what contributed to their successes in life, they rarely mention the physical setting in which they learned or even *what* they learned. Instead, they invariably recall the teachers who made a difference for them. Sometimes they talk about a stern taskmaster; at other times, they talk about someone who gave them support and nurturance with no questions asked. The teacher who was knowledgeable and erudite is as fondly remembered as the teacher who made learning fun. Because teacher quality is so important, it only makes sense that evaluating teachers and helping them grow should be a top priority for every principal.

Barriers to Teacher Evaluation

Of all the tasks that principals perform, teacher evaluation is often done the least well. Seldom do we hear teachers talk about the positive role a principal has played in their professional growth, and seldom do principals talk about the satisfaction they get from helping teachers grow. Principals rarely play the role of gatekeepers in determining who is fit to teach. During the 1997–1998 school year, for example, just 10 of Boston's 46,000 teachers were dismissed. From 1998 to 2000, only 3 of 79,156 teachers working for the New York City Board of Education were fired for poor teaching (Ouchi, 2003). Now, it's possible that the teachers working in Boston and New York are so good that only an infinitesimal number of them are unsatisfactory and warrant dismissal. I doubt it.

Despite the inherent value of teacher evaluation, there are two main reasons for the relative lack of attention that principals give to it. The first obstacle, experienced by everyone who leads a school, is that there is simply too much to do and not enough time in which to do it. The second barrier is that teacher evaluation is defined too narrowly. As a result, the relationship between teacher evaluation and teacher growth is often ignored.

> We must not be afraid of evaluation of our work. We all make mistakes and need correction, praise, and encouragement.
>
> ~Estella

Not Enough Time

There are not enough hours in the day or days in the week. Although superintendents and professors talk about the need for principals to be instructional leaders, the reality of a principal's role is quite different. Principals must create schedules, order supplies, see that schools are cleaned, counsel parents, direct students, lead faculty members, and complete paperwork. There are just too many responsibilities, too many tasks, and not enough time in which to do them all. Principals are expected to be almost all things to almost all people at almost all times. As a result, even the best principals find it hard to focus and do anything really well, particularly something as complex and challenging as evaluating teachers.

You can get a sense of the various demands on a principal's time by looking at Figure 5. I often use this questionnaire in my presentations to principals. My goal is to help them reflect on how they use their time and decide if they are comfortable with

Figure 5

How Principals *Really* Spend Their Time

Directions
- List the numbers of the four activities on which you spend the most time: ____, ____, ____, ____.
- List the numbers of the four activities on which you spend the least time: ____, ____, ____, ____.
- For each item, check off the box corresponding to High, Medium, or Low for time spent on the task.
- List the numbers of the four activities on which you *should* be spending most of your time: ____, ____, ____, ____.

Activity	High	Medium	Low
1. Communicating with parents	❑	❑	❑
2. Having negative interactions with students	❑	❑	❑
3. Having positive interactions with students	❑	❑	❑
4. Completing forms and paperwork	❑	❑	❑
5. Supervising the playground or lunchroom, or monitoring other areas	❑	❑	❑
6. Developing curriculum	❑	❑	❑
7. Dealing with maintenance or logistics issues (custodial, food service, transportation)	❑	❑	❑
8. Observing teachers and giving feedback	❑	❑	❑
9. Promoting the school's or district's image in the community; raising funds	❑	❑	❑
10. Meeting with other administrators from within the building	❑	❑	❑
11. Meeting with other administrators, not supervisors, from outside the building	❑	❑	❑
12. Meeting with central office personnel and supervisors	❑	❑	❑
13. Visiting classrooms	❑	❑	❑
14. Meeting with members of the board of education or a parent group	❑	❑	❑
15. Meeting with teachers to talk about rules or procedures	❑	❑	❑
16. Meeting with teachers to talk about pedagogy or curriculum	❑	❑	❑
17. Dealing with issues related to athletics	❑	❑	❑
18. Other (please specify): _____	❑	❑	❑

Discussion
1. Is there a disparity between how you are spending your time and how you think you should spend it? If so, why is this?
2. Has how you spend your time changed in recent years? If so, in what ways is it different and why?
3. What could you do to change how you spend your time?

their priorities. When we are busy responding to wide-ranging demands and fighting organizational fires, it's easy to lose track of priorities.

Because there are so many demands on a principal's time, teacher evaluation, despite its importance, fails to receive the attention it deserves. Many of the principal's duties have deadlines and come with a presumed urgency that cannot be negotiated. A principal can always put off an observation or reschedule a conference with a teacher, however. When this happens over time, time after time, procrastination becomes the norm and no one really expects things to be much different (including the principal).

The attitudes and behavior that result from this overload became very clear to me when I first became a principal. I worked in a medium-sized district with eight elementary schools and one middle, one junior, and one high school. Twice each month, on the morning after the board of education met, the principals would come together for a districtwide meeting. Don (not his real name) was an experienced and much-loved principal whose school was near mine. He and I would often chat after our principals' meetings, before we returned to our schools. I remember asking Don how he conducted his teacher evaluations. He rolled his eyes at me. "Teacher evaluations?" He laughed. "Who has time for them? I have a good faculty."

He shared that every spring he would walk into each classroom and say something like the following to each teacher: "I know what a super job you've been doing all year, and I haven't had the time—or felt the need—to visit or observe you. It's time for annual evaluations, though, so what if I give you a copy of the evaluation form that I have to complete, and you go ahead and put down what you think is an appropriate rating? You know your strengths and weaknesses. I'll use your thoughts when I fill out the form."

Don said that his teachers would smile and take the forms, and they would later return them to him with the rating scale

> Teachers need to evaluate their own teaching as well as the students' learning.
> ~Sharon

completed. "Basically, I use what they give me when I complete their evaluation," he said. I expressed surprise and, I'm sure, some disillusionment. "What's the big deal?" he responded. "All these teachers are good, and they are working as hard as they can. Plus, the evaluations really don't matter; after all, everyone gets the same raise. I need to spend my time on all the other stuff that I have to do."

Don's behavior spoke volumes about both the demands of his role and the attitudes that both principals and teachers often hold about teacher evaluation. I have talked with enough principals to know that few of them actually give their teachers the evaluation form to complete as Don did. But for many principals—maybe for most—the teacher evaluation process usually falls to the bottom of the get-to list.

Too Narrow a Focus

A second barrier to effective teacher evaluation stems from how we define the task. Helping teachers grow is not usually considered a part of the teacher evaluation process. Our definition of what the teacher evaluation process encompasses is far too narrow. Teacher evaluation is seen as a yes-no question: Is the teacher acceptable? If so, then the principal's time and energy are spent elsewhere.

As noted earlier by the data from Boston and New York, the working definition of *acceptable* is broad. The low incidence of teacher dismissals is the result of many factors, including state tenure laws and teachers' unions. But the way that teacher evaluation is viewed cannot be overlooked.

Typically, teacher evaluation and teacher observation are considered to be synonymous; when we talk about teacher evaluation, we mean teacher observation. Although it's true that almost any teacher observation is better than no observation (the approach employed by Don), relying solely upon teacher observations to constitute teacher evaluation is shortsighted. Doing this ignores the role of teachers in an institution and what

> I am not doing anything wrong, so why bother observing my teaching? ~Pei Jen

is needed for teachers to grow. Formal teacher observations should play an important part in teacher evaluation, but observations should constitute only one piece of a teacher's evaluation.

Formal Teacher Observations

By definition, teacher observations capture interactions between and among a teacher and her students. Meaningful observations of teachers include looking at what takes place during the lesson and the context of the lesson. That is, meaningful observations focus on pedagogy as well as instructional design, curriculum, and assessment. Even the best observations have their limitations, however.

If teachers are formally observed at all, it is probably between one and three times per year (and *if* is the relevant word). From scores of conversations that I have had with teachers and principals, it is clear that teachers who have more than a few years of experience, those with tenure, receive few formal observations. Many teachers report that they haven't been formally observed in years.

Formal teacher observations are often like Polaroid photos because they capture only a moment in time (even though the moment might be 20 or 55 minutes long). At best, the observation covers a slice of a teacher's performance. Understandably, teachers prepare with more intensity for a formal observation, and, as a result, the lesson can be somewhat artificial. Almost all teachers say that they prefer unscheduled drop-in visits, and they make a good point. A drop-in visit is more likely to reflect what happens day in and day out in a classroom. Yet there is something to be gained from formally observing a teacher, seeing a lesson that was planned with an observation in mind. Consequently, a combination of formal observations and drop-in visits is the best approach. (From my personal experience, good intentions aside, it is difficult to do unscheduled visits. Unless a

specific time and location are etched in my calendar and someone is planning on my presence, it is all too easy not to be there.)

Helping Teachers Reflect

Formal observations can be a powerful stimulus for teacher
reflection. If they are to grow, teachers need to construct meaning from their efforts both before and after an observation. That
is, teachers need to actively engage in anticipating, hypothesis
testing, reflecting, and analyzing. Whatever term is used—*reflective practitioner* or *action research* or *teacher as researcher*—the
point is the same. Good teachers do not just work from a script;
good teachers create. Good teachers plan, bringing together
their understanding of child development and the learning
process, as well as their knowledge of content area, subject matter, and pedagogy. Good teachers design opportunities for students to learn, and they assess intelligence in fair ways that also
teach. Good teachers motivate and inspire; they challenge and
support. Even the best teacher doesn't do all these things naturally. Good teachers are good precisely because they ponder,
reflect, and analyze.

Before the lesson, for example, a teacher might ask the
following:

> Last year we were observed on an informal basis and never received any write-ups. This reflected a weakness in the administration, and morale was affected. ~Bonnie

- Why am I teaching this lesson?
- What are my goals?
- What particular skills or understandings do the students
need to have when the lesson is completed?
- What do I need to do to prepare my students for this
particular lesson?
- What can I do to make it more likely that each child will
succeed?
- During the lesson, how will I know that we are all
succeeding?
- If things are not going well, what adjustments might I make?
- Which intelligences work well in this lesson?

• What will I take from this lesson to help me plan the next lesson?

• What is appropriate for follow-up and homework?

• How will I know what my students learned?

After the lesson, a teacher might consider the following questions:

• What was different from what I anticipated?

• What went well? What was disappointing?

• Which students grasped the skills or concepts and which struggled? Given what I know about these students, did their performances surprise me?

• Was the lesson too long, or did I run out of time?

• Did I ask enough higher-level, thought-provoking questions?

• Was classroom management an issue?

• Did I differentiate instruction?

• Were all racial groups and both genders equally involved in the lesson?

• How well-paced was the lesson?

• What did my students learn?

• What happens next? What should I do differently the next time that I teach this lesson?

Why does the principal walk in just when the classroom *appears* to be the most chaotic?

~Malia

Regularly thinking about such questions is an integral aspect of teacher growth. Of course, this kind of reflection can and should happen even if no observation takes place, but teacher observation can facilitate the process. Indeed, the most important aspect of an observation can be the thought and dialogue that come before and after. How a lesson becomes an opportunity for teacher growth is far less important than the fact that the thought and reflection take place.

Principals may find it helpful to share the above questions with a teacher prior to an observation. How many and which questions to share would be based on the teacher's expertise. Too many questions might overwhelm even the strongest teachers. One possible approach is to agree on which particular issues will be the focus of the observation. Will the principal be looking to see how the teacher responds to "During the lesson, how will I know that we are all succeeding? If things are not going well, what adjustments might I make?" Or will the principal be focusing on "Which students grasped the skills or concepts and which struggled?" or "Were all racial groups and both genders equally involved in the lesson?" Agreement on the focus of the observation can be addressed in a pre-observation conference or, even, through a note or e-mail that asks the teacher which issues she wants to focus on. However the agreement is reached, the questions can help frame a rich postobservation conference between the teacher and principal. Beyond this, teachers can use the questions for their own analysis, regardless of whether a formal observation occurs.

Face-to-face meetings and discussions between a teacher and principal are usually best, but a teacher's thought and reflection can be supported in other ways, too. There are a number of creative ways in which reflection and constructivist analysis can take place, some of which do not include meetings with the principal. Depending upon the principal's time and skills, the expertise and interest of the teacher, and the school's culture, one or a combination of the following strategies may be appropriate:

Glowing remarks on observations are nice but not always helpful if they are not well documented. ~Tarren

• Teachers engage in pre-observation and postobservation conferences with the principal or another administrator.

• Teachers complete pre-observation and postobservation forms that elicit their thoughts and rationale and submit them to the principal.

• Teachers from a similar grade level or subject area engage in peer observation to offer feedback and suggestions.

• Teachers from a different grade level or subject area (or perhaps from a different school) engage in peer observation.

• Lessons are videotaped, and teachers review them with peers or administrators.

• Teachers keep a portfolio that includes pre-observation and postobservation forms and videotapes of lessons.

These strategies can be supplemented by soliciting feedback from students and their parents.

Each of these approaches helps teachers focus on their performances and reflect on what went well, what was disappointing, what should be done differently, and, most important, why this was the case. Constructing knowledge of teaching skills from performance, going beyond just observing and moving to inferring and interpreting, is essential if a teacher is to grow. A teacher might be able to reflect, analyze, and synthesize on her own, but a constructivist approach requires give-and-take between the teacher and her colleagues (who may or may not be administrators).

Self-evaluation and reflection should be part of the evaluation process. ~Nelly

Assessing Teacher Performance

Because observations have such potential power for helping teachers construct knowledge, principals may want to consider developing a rubric for teacher performance. They could use this rubric when observing teachers. The rubric would help ensure that principals and teachers agree on what teaching behaviors are important and how various levels of quality are defined. Beginning with the qualities and behaviors that are listed on the district's evaluation form—descriptors such as "maintains good classroom control" or "is knowledgeable about subject matter" or "meets student needs"—principals and teachers could work together to define exactly what these terms mean for various levels of performance. The dialogue that would result from filling in the cells in a rubric (as in Figure 6) would be incredibly rich. Think of the interactions and collegiality that would come from responding to questions such as "What is the difference between a 'superior' and 'outstanding' level of 'presentation skills'?" and "What does that look like in a

	Criteria	Below Average	Average	Superior	Outstanding	Excellent
Figure 6						
Sample Teacher Evaluation Scale						
	Knowledge of subject matter					
	Knowledge of child develop- ment and the learning process					
	Presentation skills					
	Student rapport and enthusiasm					
	Professional- ism and collegiality					

classroom?" Indeed, the discussions among faculty members would be far more important than completing the actual rubric.

The rating scale in Figure 6 comes from the teacher evaluation model used at New City School. *Below average* is, as the name implies, less than satisfactory. *Average* is acceptable, nothing more. In order to remain with us, a teacher must improve beyond *average* by the end of the third year. To begin year four,

Figure Skaters and High-Divers: Why Not Teachers?

If we can determine the relative proficiency of figure skaters, high-divers, hog-callers, and square dancers, why do we shy away from making decisions about the quality of teachers? We need to do everything within our power to attract the best candidates to teaching and to help them grow and learn once they are in our schools. I believe that tying teacher pay to teacher performance can support this goal.

I am not suggesting that teachers' salaries be based on their students' test scores. I am suggesting that student progress, defined by test score results along with other indicators, should be a factor in determining teachers' pay. I am not suggesting that tying some aspect of teacher pay to merit will solve the teacher shortage problem; I am suggesting that paying teachers commensurately with their effectiveness will attract talented individuals to teaching and will help them remain in the teaching profession. I am not suggesting that developing a system of performance pay is simple or that administering it is easy; I am suggesting that talented teachers and administrators can work together to find a way to factor quality into teachers' pay. A valuable resource on the issue of performance pay is *Linking Teacher Evaluation and Student Learning* (Tucker & Stronge, 2005). The book describes several districts in which student achievement is a factor in the teacher evaluation process. The ways in which performance pay systems could be developed and administered are wide ranging. Although good teaching is good teaching, and although there are certain elements that are found in all good teachers regardless of subject matter or students, some aspects of how good teaching is defined will vary by community and school culture. If 20 school faculties developed the teacher evaluation rubrics in Figure 6, for example, although there would be strong consistency, there would also be some differences in how quality is seen. That variation is appropriate. Of course, whatever performance system is used (whatever employee evaluation system is used in any employment setting) must be administered fairly and consistently. Creating and administering a performance pay system is not easy to do. That said, it can be done if we have the will to do it.

the teacher must be rated as *superior* or better in all five areas. That is an aggressive position, but we feel that we cannot settle for average teachers. Why should we? None of us would be pleased to go to an average dentist or, even, an average auto repair shop! *Superior* implies that the teacher is performing above average, doing a good job. *Outstanding* suggests that the teacher is demonstrating many strengths. *Excellent* is the highest level of performance; it indicates that the teacher is extraordinarily skilled in the particular area. (An explanation of how New City School's performance pay plan works can be found in Appendix B.)

New Mistakes

Many of us are tempted to think that an ideal lesson is one that runs smoothly. Good teachers do anticipate and plan well, and their lessons should go smoothly. However, it is more difficult for a teacher to learn from a flawless lesson. The best learning opportunities don't come from those occasions when everything went as planned. Instead, they result from lessons when something went awry, when there wasn't enough time or there was too much time, when a student or three (or maybe the whole class) didn't get it. Granted, having too many lessons in which mistakes happen is not a good sign, but neither is an absence of mistakes.

> At my last school, they never came into my room, so I knew they really hadn't a clue as to what I did or how I was doing. I felt that they really didn't value me at all. ~Lucie

The MNM philosophy—Make New Mistakes—recognizes that mistakes are opportunities to learn. Of course, making the same old mistakes over and over isn't very smart. We should learn from our mistakes so that we don't repeat them. Yet making no mistakes isn't very smart either. Making no mistakes means that we continue to execute a familiar model or formula; making no mistakes means a lack of creativity and new strategies. Conversely, making new mistakes means that different activities and directions are being attempted. We should make mistakes when we try new things; if we don't do so, then we aren't being ambitious enough. The key is to learn from our new mistakes so that we grow as a result of them. If we want our teachers to learn from their experiences—to actively engage in anticipating, hypothesis testing, reflecting, and analyzing—they need to know that learning is messy and that it's all right to feel comfortable when they make a mistake.

This acceptance of new mistakes needs to be made explicit to all employees. If principals want their teachers to be constructivist learners, they need to be clear that they don't want to see perfection in a lesson. Teachers must be aware of the MNM philosophy and feel quite comfortable in trying new strategies. The principal sets the tone for this to happen. Before a formal observation, I will often tell a teacher, "Remember to make new mistakes. Let me see you trying something new or taking a risk." During our postobservation conference, I may begin by asking, "What new mistake did you make, and what did you learn from it?" Types of mistakes and their implications are summarized in Figure 7.

Of course, words are one thing and actions are quite another. If a principal really wants to set a tone in which MNM is practiced, she needs to demonstrate such risk taking in her own behaviors. If the MNM philosophy is to be an integral part of a school's culture, it must apply to everyone. Regardless of role, every adult in the building needs to continually try to find new and better ways to reach students. Everyone should be learning; everyone should be making new mistakes. When the principal

Figure 7	
Mistakes and Their Implications	
What kind of mistake?	**What does it mean?**
Old mistakes	We repeat our errors and do not learn from our experiences.
No mistakes	We continue to use the same approach. We are error-free, but little learning takes place.
New mistakes	We try new ideas and strategies and learn from our experiences.

shares what she learned from a new mistake that she has made, that sends a wonderfully liberating message to teachers.

Informal Teacher Observations

Dropping in on a classroom, either long enough to sit and observe or just to stop by to watch and wander around, is important. In general, by coming in unannounced, principals are more likely to see what really happens every day. Don't get me wrong; whether or not a visit is anticipated, the lesson should be good. In fact, there shouldn't be that much difference between what takes place during a formal and an informal observation. That said, teachers naturally will prepare more intently when they know an observation is going to take place. When I wander into classrooms, I try to focus on two important aspects of teaching: the rapport between teachers and students and the degree to which the lesson is designed to meet students' unique needs.

> Great observations are positive, nurturing, and focused on achieving one thing—helping that teacher gain insights into the craft of teaching. ~Susan

Limitations of Observations

Observations provide a slice of a teacher's performance, but they miss important aspects of a teacher's professional role. What happens in the classroom is the top priority, of course, but other facets of a teacher's role need to be considered when thinking about growth. What about a teacher's ability and willingness to work with newer teachers? What about the teacher's relationships with her students' parents and administrators? What about a teacher's ability to design and develop curriculum and to create assessment tools? How willing is the teacher to work with colleagues? Can the teacher hear feedback and make modifications in his behavior? These factors come together to create a full picture of the teacher as professional (and they fall under the category of professionalism and collegiality in the New City School performance pay plan, shown in Appendix B).

The principal should be involved in all these areas. Certainly, the kinds and levels of a principal's involvement will differ due to a host of factors, but as principals think about evaluating teachers, they need to consider all the stakeholders with whom the teacher interacts and all the roles that a teacher plays. (These topics are dealt with extensively in other chapters in this book. However, given their importance, I would be remiss to not at least note them in a chapter on teacher evaluation.)

Help for Struggling Teachers

The real world is quite different from Garrison Keillor's Lake Wobegone, where everyone and everything is above average, including the schools. Some teachers are going to be weak in certain areas, have difficulties, and not perform at a satisfactory level. Principals work with these teachers and give them support. That support will run the gamut, determined by the teacher's needs and the principal's resources (including resources offered by the school district). Support for the teacher may include linking him with a peer or mentor; enabling him to attend workshops, conferences, or courses; or focusing his efforts and giving him the direction and feedback that is needed. Principals need to be as supportive as possible without losing sight of the fact that their job is to help create a learning environment in which each child grows as much as possible; that means that each teacher must also grow as much as possible.

Even with the best efforts of a principal, not all teachers will grow and find success. Eventually, if a teacher doesn't meet expectations and perform at a satisfactory level, nonrenewal of his contract (or termination) is necessary. No one likes to make this decision, but there are times when it is necessary. The principal's responsibility is to ensure that children learn, not that adults have jobs.

Whenever I have an observation, something out of the ordinary happens: a spider crawls across someone's desk, I spell a word wrong on the chalkboard, the bulb burns out in my overhead projector!

~April

Unless a teacher's behavior is flagrantly egregious, many steps are necessary before a decision about continued employment is made. An ongoing process of support and feedback needs to take place in order to give the teacher an opportunity to improve. When a teacher is having serious difficulties, administrators must be explicit about the nature of the problem and equally explicit about what needs to happen in order for the teacher to receive a contract for the following year. This conversation is hard to conduct in any circumstance because we are dealing with people's livelihoods. (Of course, it is made doubly hard when the teacher in question is a caring person who appears to be giving her best efforts.)

When talking about concerns and the future, I have found that a face-to-face meeting with the teacher is essential. Regardless of how well a principal writes, regardless of how easily everyone now uses e-mail, there are some times when a meeting is necessary. This situation is one of them. Because the issues are so important, I find it helpful to have my agenda for the meeting outlined, in writing, ahead of time. The guidelines—both what needs to be said and the order in which it should be said—are shown in Figure 8 on p. 104. I use this list as a guide to help me plan for the meeting.

I find it painful to review the list because it reminds me of difficult meetings that I have had with teachers over the years. However, a principal's priority is his students, and that sometimes means making tough personnel decisions. When it's time to consider such a decision, following the steps outlined in Figure 8 actually gives the teacher the best opportunity to succeed.

Happiness Is Not the Goal

The principal's job is not to make teachers in her building happy. Teachers who are happy may be more likely to be better teachers; certainly unhappy teachers aren't going to be pleasant

Figure 8

Steps for Meeting with Struggling Employees

1. Clarify the purpose of the meeting.
   - Why have I called the meeting?
   - What specifically do I wish to discuss?
   - What particular incident or information has caused me to want to meet?
   - Is this a new behavior or part of a pattern?

2. Define expectations for performance.
   - What are the organization's standards and expectations?
   - What are my standards and expectations?
   - What should a good employee be doing? What is acceptable? (Be as specific as possible.)

3. Specify the concern that prompted the meeting.
   - What did the employee do or fail to do?
   - How do I know this?
   - Is this the first time I have discussed this issue with the employee?
   - Have I met previously with this employee about other concerns or issues?

4. Restate expectations in relation to the concern.
   - How does the employee's behavior differ from my expectations and those of the organization?
   - How egregious are the employee's actions?
   - Does the employee's behavior put his or her job in jeopardy?

5. Describe strategies for improvement (either to give to employee or to raise for discussion).
   - What can the employee do to improve?
   - How can I help the employee?
   - How can others help the employee?
   - How will the employee know if he or she is making progress?

6. Establish closure.
   - What are the next steps?
   - What should the employee begin doing differently tomorrow or next week?
   - What are the check points? When is the next time that I will meet with the employee?
   - How will I know if the employee is making progress?

7. Document the discussion.
   - Shortly after the meeting, write down what took place during the meeting for each of these steps.
   - If appropriate, send the employee a memo that reviews what was discussed and sets out what needs to happen.
   - Schedule the next meeting to discuss what progress has or hasn't been made.

for anyone to be around, whether students or peers. It is also true that a school with a happy faculty is likely to be an enjoyable setting for everyone. We all want to be liked, so it is easy for principals to want happy teachers and to want their teachers to be happy with them. However, having a goal of teacher happiness is a mistake.

The principal's goal is to create an environment in which students learn and grow. The principal does that by creating an environment in which faculty members learn and grow. If teachers are learning and growing, they will find happiness. In fact, you can often recognize a high-performing school because everyone is smiling, students and adults alike. People are smiling because of the success they are realizing. Happiness is an invariable by-product of success and achievement when *everyone* in the school is learning.

7

Facilitating Creativity and Teamwork

"The times, they are a-changing," sang Bob Dylan a generation ago. Despite the differences in the world today, that lyric is still relevant. When we think of *how* the world is different, technological advances and demographic changes come to mind. Technology that was unimaginable 20 years ago is commonplace today. (After all, the pervasive use of e-mail communication is barely a decade old.) Almost everywhere, we are surrounded by an increasing richness of human hues and backgrounds. For those of us working in organizations, these dramatic changes are rivaled by the evolution in attitudes about work, leadership, and supervision (see Chapter 3). Responding to these changes is not an option; rather, it is a mandate. The success of our schools—of our students, of our teachers, and, indeed, of ourselves—will be determined by the quality of our response.

Similarly, teaching has become far more challenging than it was in the past. Too many children come from backgrounds of poverty. Many have spent hundreds and hundreds of hours in front of a television screen, video game, or computer terminal. Teachers are constantly asked to do more. They are expected to meet their students' academic needs, to prepare them to perform well on standardized tests, and to cultivate their higher-level thinking skills. But that is just the beginning. Teachers are also expected to address their students' emotional growth and social development. Being a successful teacher requires more than knowledge about curriculum and pedagogical skills.

Successful teaching requires finding creative solutions to complex problems.

As I try to make clear throughout this book, supervising creative teachers—the kinds of teachers who make a difference in children's lives and whom every principal wants to hire—and creating a faculty that works together as a team requires a different approach to management and leadership than was the norm as little as a decade ago. In contrast to old supervisory models based on a hierarchical approach, today's leadership requires trust, collaboration, and relationship building.

Talented people in all organizations need this type of leadership, not just those who work in schools. In *The Rise of the Creative Class*, Richard Florida (2002) considers how creativity is needed to fuel the workplace (and for cities to prosper). Although his book is not about education, he describes perfectly the traits of creative teachers: "[Their] function is to create new ideas, new technology, and/or new creative content. These people engage in complex problem solving that involves a great deal of independent judgment and requires a high level of education or human capital" (p. 8). Supervision of creative individuals must evolve, Florida observes, and "traditional hierarchical systems of control [need to be replaced] with new forms of self-management, peer recognition and pressure and intrinsic forms of motivation" (p. 13). James O'Toole (1995) also captures this shift in philosophy: "With few precious exceptions, the era of the dictator, the czar, the general—even the traditional boss—has passed in Western society" (p. 5).

In discussing the changing relationship of today's supervisors and employees, management guru Peter Drucker (1999) describes *knowledge workers*, the individuals who possess "in their heads" the skills and knowledge that are needed for success. Of course, fine teachers are knowledge workers; their skills, knowledge, and artistry come from what they know, not from a workbook or policy manual. As Drucker explains,

When there's friction among the staff, you're afraid to walk around the corner. But when the staff work together well, [being at] the school is like going home. Every aspect of the job is satisfying.

~Susan

"Knowledge workers are not subordinates; they are 'associates.' For once beyond the apprentice stage, knowledge workers must know more about their job than their boss does—or else they are not good at all. In fact, that they know more about their job than anybody else in the organization is part of the definition of knowledge workers" (p. 18). If principals and supervisors want to attract and keep knowledge workers at their schools, and have them work collaboratively as a team, they need to lead in ways different from those typical in the past. Vision and inspiration are essential, but they are not sufficient.

Establishing Respect

Leaders model creativity, reward it, and make mistakes that they're willing to write off as part of the learning process.

~Kathy

Creating a school in which creativity is encouraged and in which teachers work and grow together is a challenging task and a job for which most school leaders were not trained. Such leadership requires, first and foremost, that everyone shares an attitude of respect. We often talk about the need for adults to respect students and for students to respect one another, but respect is vital to adult-adult relationships as well. All employees must treat one another with care and consideration and must respect one another. Unfortunately, as we know all too well, respect doesn't happen automatically. A good principal will institute practices that increase the atmosphere of respect.

When respect is pervasive, all people are valued as human beings and treated with dignity, regardless of their title, role, or responsibilities. Although hierarchical differences remain a reality—people do have different titles and roles, perform distinct responsibilities, and are paid varying amounts—those differences should have no bearing on how people interact with one another. This equality of treatment ranges from what people are called to how welcome they feel.

For example, a custodian or teacher's aide should be addressed by the same title as everyone else. What is the message if the principal is *Dr.* Jones and teachers are *Mr.* Simms and

Ms. Pita, but the custodian is just called Fred? Either Fred should be called *Mr.* Smith or, conversely, Dr. Jones, Mr. Simms, and Ms. Pita should be called only by their first names, Carla, Pat, and Carolyn. To use titles with some employees and not with others makes a statement about who is valued and who is not. Using proper titles may seem like a little thing, but the little things are often the big things.

Beyond names and titles, we need to ask ourselves, "Do all employees feel that they are part of the school?" What powerful messages are sent by unnecessary distinctions made due to hierarchical position? Does everyone get invited to the staff (not "faculty") parties? If staff photos are hung in the hall, is everyone's picture posted, not just those of the teachers (or, heaven forbid, only the administrators), and are the photos the same size? Is there a hierarchy within the staff lunchroom eating areas, or are all adults free to eat wherever and with whom they please? Are parking spaces allocated and reserved only for certain people? Sure, the principal may come and go during the day far more often than a teacher does, but is the cost of her having the closest parking space and walking only 10 feet to her car worth the message that this sends to everyone else? Put another way, what is the message to everyone if the principal has to find a parking space each day, just as all other staff members do?

As Suzy Wetlaufer (2000) succinctly notes, "Hierarchy never made anyone feel good, except the people at the very top" (p. 60). Too often, "little," "thoughtless" decisions like the lack of proper titles and privileged parking spaces send powerful messages that create distance among the people in an organization. "Leaders fail when they have an inappropriate attitude and philosophy about the relationship between themselves and their followers," explains O'Toole (1995, p. 37).

Respect does not have to preclude people's establishing a positive rapport with one another. In a good organization, people enjoy one another and have fun together. Dale Dauten (2003), a syndicated columnist, illustrates this point: "In every

> A true leader asks everyone to move out of his or her comfort zone, to take risks, and then allows everyone to share in the success and move forward. ~Rich

company, people are going to make fun of the boss; it's just that in good companies, it happens in front of the boss." (My reaction: *Welcome to my world!* If this is true, I must have a very, very good company!)

It Starts with Trust

Respecting one another stems from trusting one another. Does the administration trust the teachers? Is this trust shown in action, not just in rhetoric? Do the teachers, for example, have access to the supply storeroom? (The fact that I pose this question is a sad statement about schools and relationships.) If teachers do not have that access, the message is, "We trust your judgment with students but not with construction paper." Likewise, do all teachers have access to the copier and the ability to make as many copies as they deem necessary? Money can be tight, I understand, and trees are valuable. Still, if we don't allow teachers to make such decisions, how can we expect them to feel fully valued and respected? Then there is the trust that school leaders show (or don't show) about teachers' professional judgment: What roles do teachers have in selecting textbooks, developing curriculum, and determining pedagogical approaches? Here again, how can we expect teachers to feel valued and respected if they have minimal input into professional decisions?

Trust, of course, is based on interactions and experience. Do teachers earn the trust of their administrators? Do teachers take concerns or questions that they may have directly to the principal, or do they talk horizontally and spread innuendo? Do they follow through on commitments and take responsibility when they have dropped the ball, as will inevitably happen?

Trust goes both ways. A principal must earn trust from her teachers. Is she consistent in her beliefs and actions so that the teachers can accurately predict how she will react to conflict, such as when an angry parent comes to complain? Does she know when to be a conduit and when to be a buffer? When appropriate, will she be a buffer for teachers from parents and the central office? Does she keep confidences, and will she follow through on her commitments and take responsibility when *she* has dropped the ball, as will inevitably happen?

Teamwork Doesn't Happen by Accident

Working well together is not always easy, to be sure. In part, this is because the skills of working together are overlooked at every level of teacher training and development. From undergraduate teacher preparation to graduate programs to staff development offerings, adult-adult interactions receive little attention. Likewise, team building is given little attention in most administrator preparation programs. It's not terribly surprising, then, that teachers and administrators often find working as colleagues to be difficult. Tony Wagner (2001) suggests why this is the case: "With few opportunities to work with other adults during the workday, many educators have not developed the skills of teamwork" (p. 379). We cannot assume that a good faculty, even a good, *congenial* faculty, will work well together without continued direction and support from the leadership within the school. Even though the competing demands for a principal's time never end (upset parents, overdue reports, empty soda machines, and, oh yes, why aren't those test scores higher?), building creativity and teamwork within the faculty must be a priority.

Naysayers may argue that a principal does not have enough time to focus on team-building. They are wrong. Focusing on adult-adult relationships and consciously building a team is not an option for principals; rather, it is essential if a faculty is to grow and develop, work as colleagues, and create ways for students to learn. This path is not one taken in lieu of pursuing higher test scores or greater student achievement, however that is measured. This path is necessary if the adults and students are going to realize—and, indeed, surpass—their potential.

> Creativity among teachers is always there but may need a little spark to ignite it. Good administrators show teachers that thinking outside the box is not only supported but is expected! ~Sheryl

Despite the obstacles, building a team can be done. The following questions suggest some of the ways in which a principal might ensure that all work together as a team.

• Do some inservice sessions directly address how adults can and must work as colleagues?

• How is collegiality addressed in the hiring process and in new teachers' mentor meetings?

• Is congeniality, distinct from collegiality, supported by the principal?

• Are productive ways to give feedback to a teammate addressed either in faculty meetings or, as appropriate, in conversations with individual teachers?

> A good leader nurtures relationships through trust, expectations, and empowerment.
>
> ~Maggie

• Are teacher teams asked to generate team goals that will ensure collaboration?

• Is collegiality talked about and supported?

• Is collegiality part of the teacher evaluation process?

• If a teacher is critical of another teacher to parents, how is that addressed (or is such a comment even addressed)?

• If a teacher is critical of another teacher to staff members, how is that addressed (or is such a comment even addressed)?

• Does the administrator encourage and support teachers as they deal with one another on such issues?

Listening to One Another

Listening to one another is integral to respecting one another. Everyone must be given the time and the opportunity to be heard, especially in teacher-to-administrator communications. It is too easy for principals, even the best ones in the most collaborative and creative schools, to be isolated or removed from teachers' thoughts and concerns. Most principals think that this doesn't describe them, but how can they be sure? The reality is that principals are in charge, and that means that some people will be hesitant to tell them what they need to know for fear of being seen as a malcontent or complainer. Also, even though it often doesn't feel like it, people don't want to hurt principals' feelings and will withhold criticism. (Believe me, I know that it often doesn't feel like this is the case, but I also know that people really do withhold criticism.) This means that it is easy for principals to be shielded from what they need to know in order to do a good job in leading a school.

How can this dilemma be solved? Regular surveys are an essential strategy. Surveys help principals reach out and dip into the unknown. For example, each spring I use a survey to solicit feedback from my teachers on my performance. I used to distribute a form with many questions addressing specific aspects of my performance. To be candid, the responses were not all that helpful. I realized that there was a reluctance to criticize me, so asking teachers to identify my weaknesses was not terribly productive. Instead, I have found it useful to give them a survey (which they can return anonymously if they wish) that asks

1. What should Tom *start* doing?
2. What should Tom *continue* doing?
3. What should Tom *stop* doing?

These three terms—*start, continue,* and *stop*—elicit both positive and negative comments. When teachers respond, they tell me what I am doing that they find supportive and useful and what they see as not helpful. Throughout the year, I solicit feedback at other times, occasionally about a specific event or idea, sometimes more generally. Teachers can always respond anonymously to these surveys, though most of them elect not to do so. (The fact that most teachers choose not to be anonymous is helpful because it allows me to initiate a dialogue with them about their perceptions of my performance.)

Beyond distributing surveys to gather feedback, accessibility is key. Are there chances for a teacher to chat informally with the principal? Is the principal often available in the hall or teachers' lounge? Making time to be free is not easy; simply sitting

and waiting, casually chatting, is difficult. But if we want teachers to seize the moment and talk to us, we need to be sure that
the moment is there for them. This area is especially hard for
me. I understand how important it is, though, so I often go to
and remain in the lounge during the teachers' overlapping lunch
periods, even if I have already eaten. Visits to classrooms play
an important role here, too. My teachers consistently tell me
how much they enjoy my drop-in visits to their classrooms, and,
as a result, you would think that I do this regularly. Alas, such
visits are always on my list of things to do, but I never quite get
to them often enough. It is a resolution for me for next year,
however. In fact, one reason why I rely so much on formal observations (described in Chapter 6) is because if I have scheduled
time to be in a classroom, I know that I will be there. It is too
easy to be distracted and pulled away from the times when I
plan to just wander into classrooms.

Treating Employees as Volunteers

A helpful way to create a school in which the faculty works
together as a team is to think of employees as volunteers. With
volunteers, supervisors cannot rely on hierarchical (legitimate)
power to gain compliance and cooperation but must, instead,
use powers of persuasion and relationship. (See Chapter 5 for a
discussion of power.) In our desire to make a task interesting
and challenging so that a volunteer will give her time to work on
it, we must begin by knowing and understanding the volunteer.
For example, what are her interests? What are her talents? What
can we do to encourage her to give her time and energy to the
task? We must listen to her. Working with employees, people
who receive a paycheck, should be no different. We need to listen to them, too. We need to understand their interests and talents and learn what we can do to encourage them to give time
and energy to us.

Drucker (1999) observes, "Volunteers, we know, have to get *more* satisfaction from their work than paid employees, precisely because they do not get a paycheck. They need, above all, a challenge. They need to know the organization's mission and to believe in it. They need continuous training. They need to see results" (p. 21). I would add that they also need good two-way communication, and they need to be trusted. Rich and open communication, along with knowing and understanding an organization's mission, receiving sufficient training, and being supported and challenged, are just as important for an employee as they are for a volunteer. When employees are treated like volunteers, they will view their administrator as a teammate, not just a boss.

Turning Mistakes into Learning Opportunities

Because learning is messy and inefficient, school leaders must give others permission to make errors. The absence of mistakes does not mean that things are going well and that learning is taking place; indeed, it may mean just the opposite. If people are learning, they should be making mistakes. But they should be making mistakes from which they learn, reflecting upon what went wrong, and then changing their behaviors. They should not be making the same *old* mistake over and over again, and they should not continue to repeat behaviors that were not successful. They should be making *new* mistakes.

Viewed this way, mistakes are learning opportunities. We should not put a premium on a perfect performance the first time something is attempted (if we do at all). In fact, at times it may mean that principals encourage their teachers to try something new and fail, to make *new* mistakes. Sometimes, before a formal observation, I'll say to the teacher, "I am not looking for a perfect lesson. In fact, I want to see you doing something new

Teachers are more likely to take risks when they know an administrator will stand behind them and explain/defend them.

~Mary Ann

and making a mistake. When we meet afterward, we'll talk about what you learned from it." Teachers tell me that hearing this relieves a great deal of their anxiety and enables them to be creative in their teaching. I call this the Make New Mistakes (MNM) philosophy (also discussed in Chapter 6).

Creative teachers will try new strategies and be comfortable with the mistakes that come with them. Regardless of their successes (indeed, perhaps because of their successes), they will continue to experiment and seek better ways to serve students. Experimentation is promoted when principals encourage teachers to make mistakes and are supportive when they do so. The postobservation dialogue between a principal and teacher should primarily focus on questions, not judgments. Asking "What did you learn?" and "What will you do differently next time?" encourages reflection and openness. Because such questions are not judgmental, they also demonstrate that the teacher and the principal are on the same team with the same goals.

The best way for a principal to create an environment in which creativity and teamwork thrive is, no surprise here, by sharing her own mistakes and what she has learned from them. It is one thing to talk about MNM and learning from mistakes; it is another for the principal to demonstrate the value and safety of this by publicly sharing her own difficulties and mistakes and what she will do differently in the future. Sharing such experiences visibly demonstrates that she and the teachers are on the same team. This openness sets the tone for others to learn from their mistakes and creates a forum in which reflection and ongoing dialogue can take place. Because of this degree of reflection, the principal's accountability is increased and, invariably, the attitude of reflection and accountability spreads to everyone else.

In encouraging others to make new mistakes and to share them, it seems only right that I share some of my blunders with you. As I quickly and often point out, I wish that I could be as good a leader as the principals I describe. My flaws are many, and were I to recount them, this book would be far too long. I do try, however, to practice what I preach, and that includes being open to feedback and criticism and sharing my errors.

For example, a few years ago, I finally realized that our pace of curriculum renewal was too ambitious. I began an end-of-year faculty inservice by apologizing to the faculty for being unrealistic in my goals and not being sensitive enough to their needs. I have tried to learn from this experience, but, unfortunately, I continue to make that *old* mistake. Recently, a few teachers complained to me about having too much curriculum development work on their plates. I talked to other faculty members to gain a sense of how pervasive this feeling might be and became concerned that the opinion was shared by quite a number of our teachers. As a result, I distributed a survey at a faculty meeting that asked whether our curriculum development was too broad and fast-paced. Faculty members responded that this was the case, so we have cut back our curricular goals and time lines. Several teachers made a point of telling me how much they appreciated my being candid and sharing my errors and frustration. (As I look ahead, recognizing that this is a pattern, I plan to rely on input from our faculty's Curriculum Steering Committee to ensure that this old mistake isn't repeated.)

Similarly, as noted in the Introduction and in Chapter 4, we—I—do not do a good job with the goal-setting process at New City School. Each year I begin with renewed enthusiasm, vowing to give it the focus that it needs, but each year I make the same *old* mistake. Too many things get in the way, and neither the goals nor their follow-up receive the attention that they warrant. Is it any wonder, then, why some of my seasoned teachers don't place much value in this process? As a result, at a recent meeting of our Critical Friends Group (a faculty committee that meets regularly and follows protocols to discuss important issues), I shared my dissatisfaction with our goal-setting process, acknowledged that the difficulties are due to my lack of leadership, and sought input from the teachers about how we can improve. Some of the thoughts in this book about goals

Good leaders are ringmasters. They are able to look at the "madness" in each "circus ring" and pull together common ideas, important themes, and essential questions. ~Sande (especially in Chapter 4) come directly from the comments made at that meeting. (In fact, this situation was a prime motivator for me to write the chapter on goals because I knew that doing so would cause me to solicit others' ideas and to think in-depth about the process. I hoped such reflection would result in improvement. If you are curious about our progress, please send me an e-mail message.)

Creating a Setting for Growth

Integral to attracting and keeping the kinds of teachers who make a difference in students' lives is creating a setting in which everyone grows and learns. That can only happen when trust, respect, and teamwork are the norm.

> We need our relationships to be nurtured as much as our students do.
>
> ~Tamala

The creative and passionate teachers we want are not necessarily more expensive. For that matter, they may or may not have an advanced degree or be technologically savvy. What sets creative, passionate teachers apart is that they continually grow and learn. They look for creative ways to reach their students, and they look for creative ways to challenge themselves.

These kinds of teachers often aren't the easiest people to supervise, and they sometimes have difficulty working as teammates. They hold high expectations for themselves and others and are dedicated to their students, sometimes failing to see the broader context. But they are the teachers whose imprints are on the minds and hearts of our children. These are the teachers we want to attract and to keep. Fostering their creativity while building a team is not an easy task, but it must be done. When this happens in a school, everyone flourishes, children and adults alike.

Making Meetings Meaningful   8

When was the last time you heard someone say, "That was a great meeting!" or "I'm looking forward to going to this meeting"? For that matter, how often have you left a meeting feeling that attending it was a good use of your time? Most of us view faculty and committee meetings as tolerable at best. They are something that we need to attend because, well, because we need to attend them! If given the option, we would attend far fewer meetings. That is because we go to meetings anticipating how little good will come from them; we leave meetings feeling that we were right.

A bad meeting is a disservice to everyone who attends. *Bad meeting* covers a multitude of sins, but it's fair to say that most meetings are viewed as "bad" because they seem like a waste of time. Meetings usually are bad because of poor process: *how* the meeting was run, not *what* the meeting was about. Too many meetings are poorly organized and badly led, if they are organized and led at all. No matter how important and relevant the content of the meeting, poor organization leads to a frustrating experience for everyone involved (including the person who is running the meeting).

Years ago, the administrators in the district in which I was a principal were periodically summoned to meetings on school improvement. The meetings were not a good use of our time. I remember saying, "I am having trouble doing my job because I am spending all this time in meetings talking about how to do my job." Unfortunately, this experience is shared by too many people, administrators and teachers alike. Faculty and committee meetings should be productive, but that is only the beginning. They also should be settings that encourage collegiality, learning, and professional growth.

The elements that make meetings a good experience for everyone are fairly simple, almost common sense. However, that doesn't mean that running good meetings is easy. Too often, the structure of meetings isn't given enough attention. Sometimes the leader doesn't take the time to think about and plan for an effective meeting. At other times, the assumption is that because the content of the meeting is so important, the substance will carry the day. Each of these mistakes results in a bad meeting. Taking the time to plan a meeting is an investment that yields many benefits. The factors that can make a meeting successful include issues of purpose, membership, time, involvement, congeniality, physical setting, agenda, and roles.

Establishing Whether to Meet

Sometimes we meet simply because we're in the habit of meeting or because we think that we should meet. Having a meeting, after all, implies progress; at least we'd like to think this is the case. That belief is naive at best. Unless there is a genuine need to meet, meetings should not be held. Unnecessary meetings take a toll on individuals and the organization. People sitting in unnecessary meetings not only aren't getting other things done; they are being shown that their time is not valuable. In thinking about holding a meeting, our first question should always be "Is this meeting necessary?" Specifically, we need to ask, "What is the goal for the meeting, and what outcome do we seek?" Then we can decide if holding a meeting is the best strategy to accomplish the goals.

This simple test should apply to faculty meetings, too. Often, the question of whether we need to meet is not asked when faculty meetings are scheduled. We have faculty meetings because, well, just because. But faculty meetings that are used only to tell, where information is simply stated or read aloud, definitely qualify as time-wasters. They are, by definition, bad meetings. Meetings should not be held just for the purpose of sharing information; information sharing can be done in written or electronic form. If sharing information will lead to a dialogue, that is great. A dialogue, though, means give-and-take with ideas and thoughts going in every direction, not just from the leader to the group. Participants need to know that their input is important and that their efforts will make a difference. As Bandura (1997) observes, "If people believe they have no power to produce results, they will not attempt to make things happen" (p. 3).

Choosing Participants

We are always tempted to be inclusive and invite everyone to a meeting who might remotely have a need or want to attend. This is a mistake. More is not necessarily better. We need to think about the purpose of a meeting and consider its optimum group size. If meetings are to be a forum for sharing and learning, the interaction that needs to take place will limit how many people can reasonably participate. Because good meetings involve more than just listening, there is a cost to having too large a group.

The best meetings have between 4 and 12 participants. Four is large enough to yield different perspectives and allow for interplay; 12 is small enough to allow everyone to participate and be heard. Sometimes groups must be large, such as when an entire faculty needs to come together, but these kinds of meetings should not be the norm. There is an inverse relationship between the size and effectiveness of a group. Simply put, the larger the group, the less likely it is that anything meaningful will arise from its meeting.

The classroom is where I know I'm having the greatest impact. That's where my priorities are, and that's where I want to be. It often feels like meetings become a separate job. ~Ben

"Who should be at this meeting?" is a key question. Because who is at a meeting has a direct effect on the quality of the meeting, my philosophy has always been to invite people who fulfill at least one of five criteria:

1. They have knowledge or skills that will improve the product.
2. They have leadership qualities and will help the dialogue.
3. They will learn from the experience.
4. They will be part of the implementation, so they should be involved in the planning.
5. They need to be present for other reasons.

Procrastination is the thief of time. ~Laurie

The "other reasons" may be political considerations, and that is not necessarily bad. Sometimes it's wise to have someone at a meeting just because he has been *less* involved recently. Or maybe an individual is invited because she feels passionately about the issue and has been *more* involved recently. Perhaps people are invited because it would be good for them to work together, or because the cost of their not being there is higher than the cost of adding them to the group. That is OK. Clearly, who gets invited will vary depending on a host of issues. The point is to not assume membership and to be thoughtful about who is invited to each meeting.

Using Time Efficiently

Time is a finite commodity. We can manage our time better, and we can use it more effectively, but ultimately only so many minutes are available. Everyone's time needs to be viewed as a precious resource, which means that time spent in meetings must be both productive and enjoyable.

As part of my research for this chapter, I e-mailed scores of acquaintances around the world, most but not all of whom are in education. I asked them what made meetings effective and what drove them crazy about meetings. Overwhelmingly, the answers were the same: Meetings that were worthwhile were focused and crisply run. Everyone's time was respected. Meetings that drove people crazy started late, went on too long, lacked purpose, and had no clear outcome. I heard this consistently from educators, attorneys, physicians, social workers, artists, architects, and executive directors of nonprofit organizations.

Beginning on Time

Starting meetings on time is more difficult than it sounds. I say this as someone who is driven a bit nuts when he has to wait for others, but I also say it as one who, when running meetings, intentionally waits for others! I have come to realize that when I get into the habit of starting a meeting after a five-minute grace period, what I'm really saying is that the meeting starts five minutes after the announced time. I tell all the teachers who show up on time that their five minutes do not matter.

> Most meetings are like trips to get a root canal. ~Ellen

The key here is to be consistent. Start on time, and most people will respect that and arrive promptly. If people are late, it's their loss. Those who came on time should not be penalized by latecomers. (I realize the contradiction in my ways. I will do better in the future.)

Deciding When to End

Beyond the need to start meetings on time, there is the question of the appropriate length for a meeting. Again, almost all my e-mail respondents said that meetings are usually too long. No one said that meetings are usually too short. The easiest step is to limit the length of the meeting by publicizing the ending time in advance. Will the meeting end at 10:00 a.m. or 4:45 p.m.? If participants know the ending time, they will stay on task and move the discussion forward. After all, the deadline is looming.

For that matter, we should not assume that all meetings need to last an hour or even 45 minutes. An architect, Lee, responded to my question about meetings by sharing the "Blackjack formula." He wrote, "You get 21 minutes for the meeting—

that is it. After you hit 21, everyone leaves." In some companies, meetings are held in rooms without chairs. Because everyone is forced to stand, the meeting is short. True, some meetings must go longer than an hour, but those occasions should be rare. When a meeting does run this long, we need to consider attention spans and build in time for a break. Ten minutes each hour is appropriate. We also need to allow people to physically stretch and move around. Saying "Let's all stand and stretch while we talk for the next five minutes of the meeting" is a way to address these issues and yet stay on task.

Assigning Time Limits

Another way to control time is to try to anticipate which issues will take 5, 10, or 15 minutes and allocate a period of time for each item on the agenda. However, this approach has never worked for me. I have always found assigning times within an agenda to be a bit arbitrary. Instead, my bias is that at the start of the meeting, the person who is leading the group needs to raise the issue of time management and gain agreement on its importance, thus implicitly receiving permission to employ time management techniques. Too often, the facilitator simply wants to run a crisp meeting but doesn't share this information with the others. The lack of information can have disastrous consequences. Unless the participants understand why the facilitator is pushing them forward and not offering unlimited time to speakers, they may see the leader's actions as rude or controlling. When the rationale and strategies for leading the meeting are openly shared, however, participants are far more likely to give the facilitator the leeway and support she needs. When there is agreement on the process, everyone will have more of a stake in the success of the meeting.

For example, the facilitator might say, "Before we start this important discussion, let me remind you all that it's been a long day, and we don't want to be here all night. That means that I'm going to run a tight ship and move the dialogue forward, even if it means not giving you all the airtime that you'd like." Or she might specifically say to a participant, "You're making an interesting point, but I am going to have to cut you off. As I look at the clock, I see that we have a lot to cover, and we need to move on. If there is time, I'll come back later to you." Such a statement is effective because it politely limits the speaker and reminds everyone else of the time issue. Similarly, the group's awareness that the facilitator is working to stay on task enables her to say, "This is a great discussion, but I'm seeing that we have nine minutes left. Let me move, then, to the last item on our agenda, realizing that we could continue to talk about this one for a much longer time." By putting the rationale out there for all to see, the facilitator is less likely to be viewed as someone who is capricious in her leadership.

Engaging All Participants

Perhaps the most important factor in determining participants' opinions about the merit of a meeting is how engaged they feel. Are they active participants whose presence is important, or are they merely spectators? The best way to ensure engagement is by eliciting active participation from everyone. If the group is small, this shouldn't be a problem, but even if there are as few as 8 or 10 participants, it can be easy for people to simply sit and listen (or to sit and not listen). The larger the group, of course, the more likely such passive participation will occur.

   At almost every meeting I facilitate, regardless of the size of the group, I structure in a couple of times per hour when I ask a question and then give the participants time to discuss it with the one or two people sitting next to them. For example, 10 or 15 minutes after a meeting has begun, I may say, "Let me stop here and ask you to turn to the person next to you." The task I give them can be as global as "Talk about whether you like the direction in which this meeting is heading," or "Talk about two ideas we've generated that you think are worthwhile and two

Meetings should be a sharing opportunity for teachers to collaborate in a meaningful way.

~Sharon

ideas that should be scrapped," or "What has surprised you thus far about what we've done?"

Another tack is to ask for feedback on my performance: "Let me see how effective I have been at presenting this. Please turn to the people next to you and tell them what you think I said." Because the groups are so small, three to five minutes is sufficient for these discussions. What was a meeting with one facilitator interacting with one speaker becomes a meeting with one-third or one-fourth of the group talking simultaneously. After the groups talk for a few minutes, I will gather everyone's attention and ask, "Were there any common themes?" or "What did you hear that surprised you?" The point is to get everyone interacting and involved, so it is important to ask these questions in such a way that everyone participates. The small-group format takes away the opportunity for someone to just listen. Small-group discussions also increase the group's productivity because they elicit wider and richer opinions and ideas.

Having "ice-breakers," activities to help people get to know one another, is a valuable tool when the group is a new one or when it has been a long time since the group has met (such as when a faculty comes back together in August). My favorite tool is the "autograph sheet" because this activity allows people to share information about themselves and find out what they have in common with others in the group. A sample autograph sheet is found in Figure 9. A nice feature of the autograph sheet is that it can easily be individualized to particular faculties and teaching contexts by changing the items.

It is always a good idea to begin a meeting by asking a question. Starting this way helps engage everyone, even if the question is just "Who can tell me what our goal is today?" or "Who wants to share where we ended the last time we met?" or "What is the one thing we want to be sure happens at this meeting?" Some questions can also help focus the discussion and lend a positive tone to a meeting. For example, I began a recent faculty meeting by asking teachers to turn to someone sitting next to

Meetings are meaningless to me. You know that meetings are always dominated by administrative issues, nothing relevant to my own teaching.

~Pei Jen

Figure 9
Autographs, Autographs!

Directions
- Circle the number of all the descriptions that apply to you.
- Find others who have the same numbers circled. Ask them to autograph your sheet by the relevant item while you sign their sheet.
- You may collect only one signature per person.

1. Likes to sleep late   _____

2. Collects things   _____

3. Enjoys working in the garden   _____

4. Considers chocolate one of the basic food groups   _____

5. Works out at least three times per week   _____

6. Has been in the present job for at least 10 years   _____

7. Keeps a journal or diary   _____

8. Has children who live away from home   _____

9. Can't wait to have children who live away from home   _____

10. Checks for e-mail messages at least three times each day   _____

11. Would love to be a professional athlete   _____

12. Has a personal digital assistant   _____

13. Had many pets, including reptiles, as a child   _____

14. Has many pets, including reptiles, today   _____

15. Likes to read fiction   _____

16. Works at balancing the checkbook   _____

17. Drives a car more than 12 years old   _____

18. Likes to paint, sew, or work with clay   _____

19. Works in a school or district at which board meetings run past 10:00 p.m.   _____

20. Watches old movies   _____

21. Buys books from Amazon.com   _____

22. Plays a musical instrument or sings in a group   _____

23. Looks for a station with the least expensive gas before filling up   _____

24. Likes to camp   _____

25. Would like to consider a career in politics   _____

(This is not a contest!)

them and share something that is working well in their class-rooms. The dialogue was rich and spirited, and it set a nice tone for our meeting.

People must leave a meeting with a sense of accomplishment; that is a necessary part of engagement. Provide the time for a summary at the end of each meeting (one that is elicited from the group rather than offered by the facilitator). Stop the process 5 or 10 minutes early to ensure that everyone has the same sense of what happened and what will be the next steps. The facilitator should review what was presented and discussed, determine areas of agreement, identify areas where differences remain, and share what will happen next.

Engagement, if it is strong, continues after the meeting ends. People leave with a sense of accomplishment, which is a necessary part of engagement. Before the meeting ends, it is also a good idea to ask participants to give a brief evaluation of the meeting. This can be done by asking for one-word adjectives to be shared aloud with everyone or for evaluative words to be written on index cards and submitted privately. Or it can be done simply by asking, "Who would like to share thoughts about today's meeting?" My preference is actually to ask the question of the group *and* to solicit more formal feedback by getting information in writing, either on index cards or pieces of paper. Not only does soliciting feedback let the participants know that their opinion counts; the responses also can offer good feedback to the facilitator.

What gives this evaluation step real power—and empowers the group—is to begin the next meeting by addressing the information that was received: "I thought about what was said at the end of the last meeting (or "I reviewed the cards you gave me after the last meeting"), and it's clear that I moved us too quickly and didn't allow time for everyone to be heard. I'm sorry about that and hope to do better this time. If I am making that same mistake, though, will you please let me know? You can

Faculty meetings are invitations to learning.

~Angie

raise your hand and remind me, or just catch my eye and touch your nose. I'll know what you mean."

Finally, a good facilitator should always be aware of the ratio between her words and the words of the participants. Sometimes it is appropriate for the group to listen and the presenter to present. Often, however, the presenter's job goes beyond presenting. Her task is to facilitate, to help the group members grasp a common vision, to lead them to a common understanding, and to enable them to construct a new meaning. In these cases, the group members must be participants, not just observers, and the facilitator must lead the group in a way that elicits activity and involvement. At the end of a good meeting, everyone wishes that there was more time so that it could continue.

Learning from and with Peers

Faculty collegiality (Barth, 1990) is discussed at length elsewhere (Chapter 2), but it should also be noted here because it is such an integral part of leadership and meetings. After all, much of the collegial learning that takes place in a school happens at committee meetings, and sometimes at faculty meetings. We should view committees as venues for learning, not just groups for accomplishing a task. Although some committees need to address a discrete charge (formulating a discipline policy or scheduling assemblies), the best committees are those that are investigating, searching, analyzing, and problem solving. Part of the leadership role here—whether leadership is held by an administrator or by teacher-leaders—is formulating the tasks for these kinds of committees and creating an environment that supports learning. Committees and their charges that would be appropriate for almost any school include the following:

• Assessment Committee: Are there ways to capture student progress that would enable more students to succeed?

Dealing with Conflict

At times, the issues being considered in a meeting and the personalities doing the considering can come together in a volatile combination. Anticipating this, you know that a specific meeting could quickly devolve into a nonproductive, pernicious encounter. What to do?

First, the principles in this chapter—creating a setting in which people will be comfortable, listening, sticking to an agenda, monitoring time, and so on—are helpful in any meeting. Beyond that, however, you may want to consider the kiva format.

The term *kiva* is of Native American origin and comes from the Anasazi tribe of the American Southwest. It refers both to a large room used for ceremonial purposes and to a particular kind of ceremony that takes place within that space. In this version of the kiva, you set up one table, ideally a round table that has seats for no more than eight people, although the total group size can be as large as 16 or 20. (The group size should be at least double the number of seats around the table.) Those individuals without seats at the table sit in a row or rows around the table, further back, arranged in one or more concentric circles.

When the meeting begins, one of the chairs at the table is left vacant. The rules are the same as for any regular meeting, except that only the people who are sitting in the chairs at the table can speak. The remainder of the group, those sitting in the outer ring, watch and listen. To speak, they must move so that they are sitting in a chair at the table, in the inner circle. When people at the table have had their say, they leave and join the outer circle, letting someone else take their place and speak. This requirement means that the individuals who are speaking will be constantly changing.

The meeting starts with the facilitator going over the ground rules for participation. Then the leader says, "I'll begin now, but only those sitting directly around the table can speak. When one of you in the outer ring wants to participate, come and sit in this empty chair. If there is not

• Parent Communications Committee: Are there ways to reach out and involve parents that would result in greater student success?

• Community Committee: Are there ways to tap into resources, including people, in our community that could benefit students?

• Diversity Committee: Are there ways that we can do a better job of respecting the diversities of our students and staff?

an empty chair, you'll have to wait for one to open up. Those of you who are already in the inner ring, when you have had your say or are going to be listening awhile, please relinquish your chair to someone else and take a seat in the outer circle. I expect that people will be constantly moving in and out of all the chairs as they change roles from being only a listener to being someone offering comments."

As you might imagine, when issues are heated and tempers short, sometimes people are reluctant to give up their chairs and move to an outer ring; sometimes people are impatient to wait for empty seats so that they can move to them and express themselves. When this happens, the facilitator needs to remind the group that this process works only if people are considerate of one another and move appropriately.

This format offers some unique benefits. First, it allows a much larger group of people to be active participants without slowing down the conversation. A discussion with 16 or 20 people is unwieldy, but the kiva model allows that many to be engaged and to feel that they are actively participating. Although only the eight people at the table have the potential to talk, the kiva keeps participants engaged because they may move to the table at any time. Second, particularly in times of potential conflict, this model keeps any one person from dominating the conversation and increases the likelihood that everyone will participate. The facilitator can ensure this by saying, "It's been a while since there has been some movement, so how about some of you in the inner ring giving your seats to those in the outer ring?"

Tough issues can be addressed in a kiva. Its use doesn't mean that conflict is avoided, but the setup is likely to spread the dialogue among the participants and ensure that everyone is heard.

In addition to committees, another strategy for peer learning is to form a book or journal club, a group that meets periodically to discuss professional articles or books.

An essential by-product of collegiality is an awareness that everyone's efforts matter, that everyone is important, that everyone has a voice, and that everyone should be heard. Such inclusiveness cannot be overestimated. Susan Murphy (2002) notes, "Those people who feel that they are truly understood may be more likely to listen to the leader's ideas and implement his or her plans" (p. 174).

Making Time for Congeniality

Congeniality is very different from collegiality, but congeniality has a place in any good organization or productive meeting. Congeniality, in fact, forms the base from which collegiality can evolve. After all, it is much easier to work with people as colleagues if you like them. One way to facilitate congeniality is by building limited time for it into a meeting (as too much fun and play can be as deleterious as too little). The first five minutes of a meeting might be designated to New News, Update Time, or What's Happening Now. This practice allows participants to share what's going on in their lives, either with the group or the person next to them. Visibly allocating this time reminds everyone that sharing is an investment, something done to facilitate the group's productivity. (I often talk with my faculty about congeniality and collegiality, distinguishing between them and explaining why each is important. These discussions help them understand my motivations and strategies and remind them that we are all on the same team, working together toward common goals.)

> Bring coffee, and do not fall asleep while sitting next to your principal. ~Lynn

Another approach is for the facilitator to ask questions that elicit smiles and help people know one another better: "If you could have dinner with anyone alive, who would it be?" or "You just won a $10 million lottery. In 30 seconds tell me, what do you do?" This could be done at the beginning of a meeting or, even better, in the middle of a tense meeting when everyone is becoming emotionally drained. Again, not unlike the facilitator's offering an explanation for moving the dialogue along rather quickly, it is important to explain the purpose for these questions: "Let me take just a few minutes to help us unwind and get ready to deal with some tricky issues of curriculum" or "I think we need a transition before sitting around the table, so let me ask you about . . ." Sharing the rationale in this way respects the participants and reduces the likelihood that someone will feel that the facilitator is just wasting time.

Attending to Creature Comforts

Many people responding to my e-mail survey mentioned food as an important part of successful meetings. Providing something to munch on sets a welcoming tone. This is true especially if the meeting is after school, before school, during the school day, in the morning, in the evening, or on a weekend. (In other words, food is always a welcome addition to any meeting!)

A synergy evolves when meetings bring faculty and administration together as equal learners aspiring to attain agreed-upon goals.
~Rich

The physical setting also can be very important in determining the productivity of a meeting. People need to be comfortable—but not too comfortable. (I would not want to lead a meeting in which the participants were in reclining chairs!) Too often, we simply meet in the space available or assigned, and we don't stop to think about what might be gained by meeting in a different location, by sitting in different chairs, or by rearranging the furniture. How do the dynamics of the group change when sitting at a long, rectangular table versus sitting around a circular one? What happens if a meeting is held in a classroom rather than in the conference room or in the principal's office? How do things change if an after-school meeting takes place off-site, at a coffee house?

Some answers are obvious. For example, it is always better when participants can see one another's faces; unless the group is too large, a circular table offers advantages. Other answers will depend upon the group and task. What is important is that we consider these kinds of issues and not take them as givens that cannot be changed.

Creating the Agenda

Every meeting should have an agenda that not only states why the group is meeting (the goal) but what will happen (the activities or issues to be discussed). Again, a failure to share this information with the group allows participants to infer that something is being done *to* rather than *with* them.

One way to reinforce the sense of collaboration—*We're all in this together!*—is to give everyone an opportunity to create the agenda. For virtually all meetings, any participant should be able to add something to the agenda. The facilitator or person in charge of the meeting may, in fact, create the agenda, but that does not mean that she should have a monopoly on it. The agendas can be public (written on a dry-erase board so that anyone can offer an item simply by writing it on the board), or the leader can make it known that items can be given to her for inclusion. This collaboration is especially important for faculty meetings. Posting the agenda—having it visible so that everyone can see it or distributing it on a sheet of paper—increases the likelihood that the discussion will stay on task. An agenda empowers the facilitator by ensuring that everyone understands the goals of the meeting.

A leader models deep listening and seeks to understand. ~Mike

Allocating Roles

Another effective strategy, particularly if a meeting has the potential to be difficult or contentious, is to formally assign roles to the participants. Although many of the roles described below are typically performed by the facilitator, assigning them to others does not diminish the leader's role. Instead, participants are more likely to be active and invested in the success of the meeting and be helpful to the leader. These roles may include

- taskmaster, the person who keeps the group focused;
- timekeeper, the person who ensures that time is used efficiently;
- herder, the person who clarifies, rephrases, and seeks consensus;

• energizer, the person who offers positive reinforcement and is concerned about the well-being of the group; and

• devil's advocate, the person who looks at things from other perspectives and asks the difficult questions that may be overlooked.

Depending upon the size of the group, more than one person can be assigned to the same role; conversely, not every person needs to be assigned a role. The assignments can be done randomly by drawing names, or the facilitator can assign them. Sometimes it is valuable to assign people to roles that are quite different from those that they normally play.

It is a good idea to publicly acknowledge the roles that people are playing. For example, give participants an index card stating their role and have them place it in front of them or wear it as a name tag. An alternative is to assign the roles privately before the meeting and announce only the roles, not the players. The facilitator can set aside time at the end of the meeting for participants to identify who was asked to play which role. This task causes everyone to pay special attention to the flow of the meeting and the roles that are being played, which never hurts. Another strategy that is helpful in engaging participants and gaining an investment in the process is rotating the facilitating duties among the group members.

> Good leaders keep the bar high yet offer ways for one to individually grow. ~Sande

Increasing Productivity

The productivity of faculty and committee meetings can be a key factor in improving both the quality of a school and the professional development of the participants. Bad meetings—meetings that aren't a good use of time—do more than waste time and energy.

There is an opportunity cost to bad meetings as well, the cost of things that don't happen because people are stuck in meetings that yield no progress. The suggestions I have offered can make meetings more productive and enjoyable. Although the details will vary with group and purpose and context, one constant remains: The facilitator must respect the members of the group. They, after all, are giving their time and skills to be part of a joint effort. It is the facilitator's responsibility to use this setting both to accomplish the goal and to help everyone grow.

Celebrating Our Differences

9

Recently, I gave a presentation to a group of educators about New City School. In describing the school, I stated, "We value diversity and are pleased that 34 percent of our students are minorities, students of color." During the break, one of the audience members, a blind woman, came up to congratulate me on valuing diversity. She also chastised me for talking about diversity solely in racial terms.

"What about me and others who have a physical disability?" she asked. "Don't we have minority status?"

I recognized that she was correct and apologized to her. She was accompanied by a friend, who then reminded me that religion can also be a form of diversity. "And don't forget sexual orientation," she said. I nodded because, of course, they both were right.

Too often, we fall into the trap of equating the term *minority* with *people of color*. We say "minorities" when we talk about people whose skin color is not white. Such language is not only incomplete and inaccurate, but it is also offensive to many people. When we speak only to race, we are ignoring all the people who are different from the majority in other ways and the implications that follow from their diversity.

For that matter, even if we think only of race, people of color are not a minority. Worldwide, there are more people with a darkened skin color than without, and, as noted later in this chapter, this soon will be the case in the United States as well. In addition, the term *minority* suggests that there is a majority, that there are only two groups. When applied to race, this is not the case. There are many different hues of skin and racial categories. Unfortunately, the term *minority* ignores those differences by lumping all non-Caucasians into one group. That broad brushstroke fails to recognize and appreciate the differences, both inherent and cultural, among us. It also seems to imply that somehow the "minority" race needs to be assimilated into the majority race.

Finally, as was pointed out to me, when we use the term *minority* to refer only to skin color or race, we are ignoring many other different kinds of groupings that can be separated into minorities and majorities. Skin color is the easiest to note because it is so visible. In addition, legislation, policies, and judicial actions in education have often addressed racial discrimination, so it is only natural that race comes to mind when we think about diversity. Yet there are far more diversities than race in society and in our classrooms.

People should be recognized and respected for who they are individually, who they are as defined by the characteristics they possess, and who they are as part of the groups to which they belong. At a minimum, when we think about diversity, we need to consider not only race but gender, religion, physical challenges, economic status, age, disability, sexual orientation, and learning differences. Indeed, some people define themselves not by their race but by one or more of these other descriptors.

Although every individual needs to be cognizant of these issues and treat all others with respect, school leaders have an even greater responsibility. Because of our positions, we set the tone and we are the role models. We need to be conscious of our actions and recognize that in this area, in particular, what we fail to do can send a message that is as powerful as any action we might take.

> We tend to categorize ourselves and others continuously. Though this endless process of categorization is part of how we all develop, we must not forget that no one can be excluded. ~Ben

The U.S. Numbers

We often say that we cannot predict the future with any degree of accuracy, but that is not the case when it comes to racial demographics and school enrollment. After all, today's kindergartners were born five years ago; those born today will start school in five years. This is not higher math! As I stated earlier, the numbers tell us that the term *racial minority* will soon lose its significance. According to the Census Bureau, minority groups will constitute 49.5 percent of the population in 2050 (Armas, 2004, p. A1). Further, by 2050, Hispanics will increase their ranks by 188 percent to 102.6 million, or roughly one-quarter of the population (p. A2), and blacks will become the second largest minority.

Other diversities are not easy to count, but the difficulty in tallying does not mean they are not present. Conventional wisdom suggests that 10 to 12 percent of the population is gay or lesbian. Therefore, every school likely has gay or lesbian staff members. We know that as many as 15 to 20 percent of students may have some type of a learning difference. Even though successful people accommodate for these differences and overcome them, that doesn't mean that they disappear upon reaching adulthood. Thus, even considering that teachers are, by and large, people who enjoyed attending school and were successful, it seems reasonable to estimate that 10 percent of staff members may have a learning difference. Similarly, people's economic status, physical disability, and religion will vary, but rarely will a school be without diversity in these areas. Even if a school staff or student body lack diversity, understanding and appreciating the various diversities still must be made a priority.

Inevitably, this means that tomorrow's schools will be much more racially and ethnically integrated than is the case today. Although other forms of diversity may not increase numerically or as a proportion of the population, it is just as inevitable that

Be part of the kaleidoscope, and celebrate the beautiful picture. ~Laurie people's acceptance of them will increase. A good example of this is the fact that today some, although certainly not all, high schools sponsor support groups for students who are gay and lesbian. As recently as a decade ago, this acceptance and public sanction would have been unimaginable. The struggles for respect and equal rights are far from over, and the gains are often incremental. Yet if we look back and reflect upon the progress that has been made, it is clear that the gains will continue.

Progress will at times come slowly and painfully, but it will come. The need for progress makes it essential that principals play a leadership role in both their schools and communities and work to create an environment that goes beyond tolerance. School leaders must create a setting in which there is an *appreciation* of diversity. We need to do so not only because it's "the right thing" to do, which it certainly is, but also because doing so is no longer an option. In tomorrow's world, virtually every setting will contain a range of hues, backgrounds, disabilities, and attitudes. As we think about how to prepare our students to succeed, it is imperative that we prepare them for that diverse world.

> Human diversity is often quoted but seldom internalized. The 21st century begs for an understanding among peoples and cultures. We have a mandate to teach our charges the importance of attaining this understanding with an open mind and a willingness to challenge old beliefs.
>
> ~Rich

Diversity in Schools

New City School has gained considerable attention as a multiple intelligences (MI) school. Hundreds of educators visit us each year, and our work provided much of the inspiration for my book *Becoming a Multiple Intelligences School* (Hoerr, 2000). Before we discovered MI in 1988, however, we were known for our appreciation of and focus on diversity. Today, after implementing and celebrating MI, we are still known as a school that embraces diversity.

Demographically, New City School is quite diverse. In 2004–2005, for example, 34 percent of our 360 students were students of color; 28 percent of our students, students of all colors, received need-based financial aid. A significant number of our students, probably 10 to 15 percent, learn differently. (Success for many of these students is increased because we frame our curriculum and instruction through MI.) A number of different religions are evident in our student body, and quite a few of our students come from families in which their parents are openly gay or lesbian. Despite the fact that we provide no transportation, we enroll students from 52 different zip codes.

My staff of 56 includes 12 people of color and 8 males (men represent a form of diversity in an elementary school). Of these 20 people, 12 are faculty members. However, these numbers only set the stage for our efforts with diversity. In presenting what schools might do to support diversity and create a climate in which all staff members and students are comfortable, I will draw upon some of my experiences at New City School.

The ability to deal successfully with issues of diversity is enhanced when a school's students and staff are diverse. A diverse student body and staff bring a variety of experiences and perspectives to issues of diversity and discrimination, and everyone in the building benefits because of this. However, numbers alone are not sufficient; it is not enough to have diverse students and staff, as important as that can be. Enrolling students who represent many diversities and having a sizeable percentage of racial minorities—whatever those minorities are—is only a piece of the diversity puzzle. (I specifically mention racial minorities because, as noted, many of our country's judicial and legislative efforts have addressed race, the No Child Left Behind Act being a recent example.) Numbers are important, but what happens once the children and adults walk through the school's doors is even more important. That is where school leaders make a difference.

School Leadership and Diversity

Too often, diversity efforts in school focus only on the formal curriculum and only on students. Although a school's curriculum is an integral part of its efforts to embrace diversity and students should be the focus of every school effort, diversity efforts will not be effective unless the entire school milieu is considered. School leaders must address the diversity climate in their schools in four distinct ways.

1. They must ensure that diversity issues are an integral part of the formal and informal curriculum and are focused on throughout the year (not only in February, during Black History Month).

2. They must pay attention to the physical setting and mold it in a way that raises awareness, educates, and offers comfort to everyone, especially those who represent diversity.

3. They must work to help all the adults in a school community become more comfortable with and appreciative of one another.

4. They must continually show their personal commitment to diversity.

The Formal and Informal Curriculum

Often, when we make plans and create strategies, we limit ourselves to focusing on the formal curriculum. Equally powerful messages emanate from the informal curriculum. In fact, a good case can be made that most powerful messages come from a school's informal curriculum.

The informal curriculum consists of the routines, practices, policies, and culture that guide our behavior; it is what we *do*. We may teach that the U.S. Constitution holds that all men are created equal, but what do our actions say about how we value individuals who are gay or lesbian? We may teach that the Holocaust was a terrible event, but does our school accept and support a range of religious beliefs? Is this respect evident when looking at events and holidays in the school calendar? We might say that we value human diversity, but what do the papers and work samples on the bulletin boards and walls indicate about which kinds of students and behaviors are esteemed? We may say that all individuals warrant respect, but are all the members of our staff treated with equal dignity? Such examples represent the informal curriculum, which guides attitudes and behavior. The messages sent by the informal curriculum are very obvious, and regardless of age, students (and their parents) are savvy at watching what we say and comparing it to what we do.

The formal curriculum is what we *say*. It is what is in a school's scope and sequence documents, curriculum guides, and textbooks. Report cards reflect progress made with the formal curriculum. The formal curriculum indicates at which level students study the efforts of Martin Luther King Jr., at what grade they learn that Columbus didn't really discover America after all, and in which classes they talk about bigotry and the Holocaust. Teachers and principals share the formal curriculum at open houses and parent-teacher conferences. The formal curriculum is so important because it determines the content that will be addressed and for which teachers will be accountable.

> People in power have a responsibility to recognize and embrace the differences among us. They cannot be ignored. ~Tamala

Diversity should be addressed throughout our curriculum as we seek to promote an understanding and awareness of one another. At New City School, for example, diversity is an integral part of each grade's curriculum. Our 5th graders take three field trips to the first cemetery in Missouri that was dedicated to black slaves. While there, our students engage in community service by helping to clean the grounds. They also learn about the history and the culture that went into creating this cemetery. Why was there a separate black cemetery? How did these people live? What can be learned from what is written on the tombstones and in other documentation? What attitudes might be reflected by what is written?

Similarly, when our 3rd graders study Native Americans, they do it from a much richer perspective than basic U.S. history. The differences between the Native American tribes and the U.S. government are seen in the context of different cultures and how those cultural beliefs influenced attitudes and behaviors. Likewise, the differences among the Native American tribes are used as a way to help students see and understand differences in lifestyles, homes, traditions, and attitudes. Looking at these questions through a Native American perspective as a 3rd grader sets the stage for looking at the civil rights struggle as a 5th grader.

I could offer more examples from every one of our grades, and each would reinforce the same point. It is easy to view social studies as a compendium of facts and information (and particularly tempting to do so when test scores play such an important role in how schools are perceived), but doing so ignores the unique role that history and geography can play in raising and addressing issues of human diversity.

Students need to learn that man's actions (*man's*, intentionally) in passing legislation, maintaining traditions, and waging wars invariably reflect negative attitudes about others who are different. We can see this in the lack of opportunities available to women and those not born into wealth, and we can study this in the civil rights movement, the woman suffrage movement, the Irish Potato Famine, the history of U.S. immigration policies, and the Japanese internment camps. Unfortunately, the list goes on and on.

The difference I perceive in my fellows enriches me. ~Brian

Regardless of the topic or era being studied, every teacher has an obligation to raise and support issues of human diversity, as appropriate. Granted, it is definitely easier for a social studies teacher than a math teacher to do this, just as it is easier for a teacher of literature than a chemistry teacher. The math and chemistry teachers may have to work harder to find nontraditional mathematicians and scientists (those who are not Caucasian males) who made a difference. But just as every teacher takes it as a personal responsibility to teach the scholastic skills and understandings that students need, each teacher needs to recognize the responsibility to help students understand and appreciate others who are different from themselves.

The formal curriculum must include an understanding of prejudice and discrimination, both historically and today. For example, is the Native American Trail of Tears journey studied in U.S. history? How might the actions of Rosa Parks be compared to those of Sir Thomas More? Do students learn that discrimination, in many forms, is still a part of life in the United States? In a developmentally appropriate way, it is essential that the formal curriculum address these kinds of issues and that students learn that there are multiple perspectives on every issue. It is also important that they learn that each of us has a role in helping make the world a better place.

School leaders must ensure that both the informal and formal curricula reflect an awareness of diversity issues and considerations. They can accomplish this by helping faculty members understand how important it is, by referring to diversity issues before and after classroom observations, and by asking questions that lead to faculty introspection.

Finally, although I have focused on curriculum, it is important to note that not only *what* we teach but also *how* we teach has implications for diversity. Our instruction should support another diversity: the recognition that people learn in different ways. The works of Carol Ann Tomlinson (2001), for example, or Robert Marzano (2001) and colleagues offer varied approaches to achieving this differentiation, as does the implementation of Howard Gardner's theory of multiple intelligences (Faculty of the New City School, 1994, 1996). Whichever model of curricular and instructional differentiation is embraced is far less important than having differentiation be the expectation.

> I like to know that a leader will look at all sides of an issue and will not be ruled by his or her emotions.
>
> ~Mary

The Physical Setting

Years ago, the New City School Board of Trustees was discussing our efforts to support diversity. At one point, a black board member asked, "This is all well and good that we value diversity, but what message would I receive if I were in the school at midnight? Would I know how much our school values diversity?" We were all silent for a moment, stunned by her questions.

This board member had pointed out a lost opportunity. For although our walls and halls were adorned with student work—work that was of high quality, work that was definitely "in progress," and work that represented all the intelligences—there wasn't much that spoke directly to our appreciation for and our efforts toward diversity. Our intentions for diversity were pure, but this wasn't reflected in what we posted and what we shared. This realization led to a fascinating discussion on the need to ensure that our values were apparent in our building at any time of day or night.

Today, one of our stairwells has a giant diversity mural (approximately 30 feet by 15 feet). The mural was created by our students under the direction of our art teacher, and it portrays people who have overcome discrimination of various sorts. Mahatma Gandhi is featured there, as is Helen Keller. So, too, are Harriet Tubman, Franklin D. Roosevelt, Martin Luther King Jr., Louis Braille, and Miriam Oldham, a St. Louis civil rights activist. One cannot walk down our hall without being struck by the dedication of space and the power of the image. But that is just the beginning.

We have learned that it is not enough for the halls to entertain; they must also affirm, and they must educate. Every student, faculty member, parent, and visitor who walks down our halls learns a bit about us and sees what we value. We use these spaces to show that we believe in MI and that our students are smart in many different ways. We also proclaim that we value human diversity and show some of the things that we do to develop this diversity in our students. We have learned that posting students' work does not suffice, however rich it may be; we must also offer an explanation. As a result, every display of student work posted in our halls is accompanied by a narrative. This explanation offers the rationale for the exhibit and helps the reader put the students' efforts into context. The displays educate the reader. Recently, for example, the following displays were posted in our halls:

> Soon we will understand that the human diversity inside the classroom is not a problem; it's a solution. ~Monica

• A bulletin board that compared kindergarten students' skin colors to the colors of familiar materials (brown sugar, bran flakes, cocoa, bananas). The students' names were placed beside the colors in a vertical array, which became a bar graph. This activity and display took students' range of skin color and made it a comfortable and discussable topic.

• An analysis of a poem about deer hunting. Half of the students wrote from the perspective of the deer and half from that of the deer hunter. An important part of preparing students to live in a diverse world is to help them "appreciate the perspectives of others, particularly those of other races and cultures." (This wording comes from the first page of our report card; it is something on which we assess our students.) It is easy for children to think of every deer as Bambi, so causing them to look at this situation from the perspective of the hunter forces them to widen their thinking.

• A photo display of student-created puppet shows that captured some of the tensions in the U.S. South prior to the Civil War. Students were given three characters—a slave, a slave owner, and a free person who helped slaves—and were asked to write dialogue that depicted issues that they would have discussed and how they would have felt.

• Murals accompanied by written pieces that illustrated one of the "isms" (racism, sexism, ageism, or lookism, which refers to when people are discriminated against because of their physical appearance). Students used their spatial intelligence to show the discrimination happening and then wrote about how they felt.

The Adult Community

Although curriculum and students should be an important focus, we cannot ignore the human context in which curriculum is taught and students learn. When we think about what must be done to create an environment in which everyone feels safe, comfortable, and appreciated, we must consider all the members of a school family. Our efforts toward diversity must include all the adults in the building, even those who rarely enter the doors.

This belief is not unlike Barth's (1990) contention about faculty collegiality: If we want the children to grow and learn, the adults must grow and learn (discussed in Chapter 2). Similarly, if we want our students to understand their differences and appreciate one another, the adults in the building must understand their differences and appreciate one another. Such appreciation is, alas, much easier said than done. Personal values and political leanings aside, adults are often far less comfortable than children are in dealing with issues of diversity or race. (Of course, this unease makes it almost impossible for them to address issues of diversity or race with their students.) In addition, sometimes such efforts meet opposition from the faculty because "That is not what we're here for" or "We don't have time for these kinds of games" or "My job is to teach children how to . . ." As school leaders, however, we cannot let this reluctance deter us from our goal. If we want a school environment that prepares students for an increasingly diverse world, we have an obligation to work on issues of diversity with all the adults in our school.

Faculty. There we were at an inservice meeting, all our faculty members standing in the gymnasium in a large circle, maybe 60 feet in diameter. Linda, one of our teachers and the chair of our faculty's Diversity Committee, stood in the center and led us in a social identifiers activity. "This is a silent activity," she said. "There will be a time to talk later. I'll read all the categories within a grouping so that you can hear them, and then I'll read them a second time. After that, please move to the spot that best describes you in relation to the category." She announced a title and began to read different categories within that group, pointing in a wide arc around the room. On her second reading, when we heard a description that most accurately fit us, we moved to that part of the circle.

After announcing the category of birth order, Linda read the choices. "Stand there," she announced, pointing to her left, "if you are the oldest child in your family." She paused. "Stand over here," she said, pointing a bit to the right, "if you are a middle child." Pointing straight ahead, she continued, "Now stand here if you are the youngest child and stand over there if you are an only child. Stand on my far right if you are neither the oldest, nor youngest, nor middle." She waited a moment. "Look around. Notice who is part of your group. Notice who is not. Think about how you feel being a part of the group." It was interesting to distribute ourselves and fascinating to see who went in which group, who was in the same group, and how some groups were quite large and others very small.

We sorted ourselves by comfortable categories like hand dominance and birth order; we also addressed tougher issues such as religion, the socioeconomic status into which we were born, and the socioeconomic status in which we currently place ourselves. Examples of categories that can be used in this exercise are found in Figure 10 on p. 150.

I was surprised a few times at how individuals identified themselves on certain issues. Once, a teacher with whom I had worked for years placed herself in a different racial category than I expected. This sorting process was repeated more than a dozen times, taking about 30 minutes. As noted, we were not allowed to talk during this exercise. The silence kept us on task and also allowed a myriad of reactions and questions to ferment in our minds. I remember thinking that I really wanted to talk with someone about what was happening.

After we had sorted and resorted ourselves, the next step was meeting in groups of five. We were given an hour and 15 minutes to debrief what we saw and felt and to speculate about the implications for us as educators. When Linda gave us this assignment, I remember thinking, *Seventy-five minutes? We don't need that much time—and I have other things to do!* I was wrong.

Leaders inspire confidence, are flexible, and bring out the best in others. Number one, though, I think, is inspiring confidence. ~Kathy

---

Figure 10

Social Identifiers Activity

Hand dominance:
- right-handed
- left-handed

Regional identification:
- Northerner
- Southerner
- Easterner
- Westerner
- Midwesterner
- Southwesterner
- New Englander
- from another country

Race:
- African American or black
- European American or white
- Latino or Latin American
- Middle Eastern
- Multiracial or biracial
- Native American
- Pacific Islander
- South Asian

Age:
- 20-something
- 30-something
- 40-something
- 50-something
- 60-something
- 70-something

Religion:
- atheist
- agnostic
- Buddhist
- Christian
- Hindu
- Jewish
- Muslim
- Zoroastrian
- nonpracticing
- other

Birth order:
- oldest child
- middle child
- youngest child
- only child
- neither oldest, youngest, nor middle child

Socioeconomic situation growing up:
- low income
- working class
- middle class
- upper middle class
- upper class or wealthy

Socioeconomic situation today:
- low income
- working class
- middle class
- upper middle class
- upper class or wealthy

Gender:
- male
- female

Vision:
- glasses or contacts
- no glasses or contacts

Family structure growing up:
- nuclear family
- single-parent family
- family of divorce
- blended family
- extended family (being raised by a grandparent or other relative)
- family with another configuration

Family structure today:
- nuclear family
- single-parent family
- family of divorce
- blended family
- extended family (living with a grandparent or other relative)
- family with another configuration

Eating habits:
- vegetarian
- kosher
- meat eater or nonvegetarian
- vegan

Familiarity with gays and lesbians:
- Someone in your immediate family is gay, lesbian, bisexual, transgender, questioning.
- Someone in your extended family is gay, lesbian, bisexual, transgender, questioning.
- A close friend is gay, lesbian, bisexual, transgender, questioning.
- One or more acquaintances are gay, lesbian, bisexual, transgender, questioning.
- As far as you know, no family member, friend, or acquaintance is gay, lesbian, bisexual, transgender, questioning.

Able-bodiedness:
- not now or not always fully able-bodied
- always fully able-bodied

In fact, precisely because we had more than an hour, we talked and talked and talked. There were some awkward silences, but they led to productive interactions. Because we had so much time to talk, we moved beyond the superficial ("I was surprised to see that there were so many vegetarians") and were able to talk about some significant issues. We discussed, for example, how it affects our faculty that so many of us came from intact homes. Are we perhaps less sensitive to children of separation and divorce? Or are we overly sensitive?

We also wondered about the implications of so many of us being the oldest child in the family. Most of the faculty members were raised in a middle-class setting, and we talked about how this might affect how we deal with families who are from wealth or poverty. Race was a topic, and we talked about the racial composition of our staff and student body in comparison to the racial contexts where we grew up, went to school, and live today. We talked about the various categories that were called out and speculated on how difficult it might have been for others to self-identify. We also shared how, occasionally, it was hard for us to do so. There was a higher comfort level in sharing in the small group than was present in stepping out in front of everyone.

Afterward, I talked to individuals who met in different groups, and there was one constant: All the conversations were fascinating and open. This social identifiers activity caused us to look at one another in different ways, facilitating our appreciation and understanding of one another. It also set the stage for us to talk about our backgrounds and characteristics, both the salient and the hidden, and their possible influence on us as individuals and as educators.

As productive as this activity was, we made a mistake in doing it only with teachers and administrators. Several of us agreed that we had missed an opportunity by not involving the rest of our staff. Better late than never, we repeated the process a few months later with our remaining staff members. Once again, I participated, but the teachers who had taken part in the activity in the spring did not. The goal remained the same: raising differences in a positive way and helping us begin to understand and accept one another. Their feedback about the activity was equally positive. Later, we did this activity with members of our board of directors, mostly noneducators, and the results were also quite good.

I don't mean to overestimate this activity; after all, it was but a couple of hours during one inservice session. I cite it here, though, because it stems from an attitude that all school leaders need to have. Once we recognize the importance of pushing diversity issues with adults, it is our responsibility to find ways to help our staff grow in this area. As in so many other areas, though, even the best school leader needs the assistance of others. I have found that an active faculty Diversity Committee is essential in this quest. At New City School, this group helps frame the inservice activities that support diversity (planning the social identifiers activity, for example), talks about issues of diversity and how our school can improve, and often supports a diversity book club. Last summer, the group chose *The No. 1 Ladies' Detective Agency*. During the previous summer, we read *Boys and Girls Learn Differently* and *A Mind at a Time*. The group has also read *Why Are All the Black Kids Sitting Together in the Cafeteria?; Daughters; White Teacher; Warriors Don't Cry;* and *I Know Why the Caged Bird Sings*. These titles were also noted in Chapter 2 when I discussed forming a book group as a tool to pursue collegiality. Collegiality is always the goal, but sometimes a title is chosen that also furthers our appreciation for and understanding of an issue, in this case diversity.

Staff. With diversity issues, as with so many other areas, our staff members are crucial to our success. They represent the front line in dealing with students' parents; they often interact with our students; they always deal extensively with faculty members. They need to know that an understanding and appreciation of human diversity is important. This means that they

A faculty should love, learn, cry, play, and grow together. ~Angie should be included, as appropriate, in inservice activities. Although it doesn't make sense to have a secretary and custodian attend a presentation on teaching phonics or preparing for AP tests, it does make sense to include them in any dialogue that addresses diversity.

We need to consciously include all staff members in holiday parties, showers, birthday celebrations, and the like. One of my favorite philosophers and authors, J. K. Rowling, notes this in *Harry Potter and the Goblet of Fire* (2000). When speaking to Harry Potter, Sirius says, "If you want to know what a man's like, take a good look at how he treats his inferiors, not his equals" (p. 525). I find the word *inferior* objectionable, but Sirius's point is a valid one. We must make our staff members, typically the lowest paid people with the least glamorous jobs, feel valued, respected, and appreciated.

Parents. Parents need to understand how hard a school is working on diversity, and they should be invited to be part of the effort. For years, for example, we have hosted a Diversity Dinner and Dialogue (DD&D). The motivation for this dinner stems from the realization that working and playing with others of different races is usually easier for our students than it is for their parents. Most of our students' parents grew up in segregated areas, and most of them work and live in settings that are not especially diverse, certainly not as diverse as our school. The DD&D started with the recognition that despite their differences in skin color and economic status, our students' parents and our staff members often share similar interests.

Parents and staff members were invited to come for dinner and chat about issues of their choosing. On each table was a large sign to indicate what would be discussed that evening. Choices included politics, sports, gardening, automobiles, cooking, travel, books, working out, movies, and hobbies. Parents chose a topic/table and chatted over dinner. Note that racial relations was not offered as a topic. We felt that this topic would be on everyone's mind, given the stated purpose of the evening, and we didn't want to inhibit conversation by offering a potentially contentious issue. Of course, people at many of the tables did wind up talking about race in one way or another.

The DD&D was a wonderful success. Afterward, people told me that they really enjoyed talking in-depth to others who were of different races and backgrounds than they were. Many of these same people, of course, had seen one another in the halls or stood next to one another on the soccer sidelines for years.

After a few years of using the DD&D to facilitate conversation, the event evolved to inviting speakers to talk with parents, faculty, and staff about issues of diversity over dinner. These issues ranged from Jew-Arab relations in the Middle East, to responding to 9-11, to segregation in the United States, to gays and lesbians. Recently we began to offer a second diversity event each year for parents, with more of an entertainment focus.

A couple of years ago, our faculty Diversity Committee planned an inservice day to address gay and lesbian issues. A panel composed of New City School parents who are gay or lesbian spoke with the faculty about what it was like to grow up homosexual. I share this information here, in talking about building relationships with students' parents within the context of diversity, rather than in Chapter 10, which deals with parental involvement, because we used the activity as a tool to let our parents know what we value and what we do.

The morning of the inservice session, prior to hearing from the panel, our faculty confronted a large sheet of paper, divided into a grid. The purpose was to elicit our personal experiences and comfort levels with people who are gay or lesbian. We were each given small adhesive circles and were asked to place them in the cells that best described our experiences with gays and lesbians. The categories are shown in Figure 11.

Responding to this simple chart accomplished two important purposes. First, it set the tone for the day by causing each of us to reflect on our own experiences and by enabling us to see how we compared to others on our faculty. Second, after the

> We've discovered we need a "Civility Plan"; we need to offer respite for the generally positive people from the generally negative.
>
> ~Barry

Figure 11		
Interactions with Gay and Lesbian People		
I do not know anyone who is gay or lesbian.	I know people who are gay or lesbian.	I have a family member who is gay or lesbian.
There are gay and lesbian members of my religious community.	I have gay and lesbian neighbors.	I am close to someone who is gay or lesbian.

inservice day was over, this large piece of paper was posted in our front hall for our students' parents to see, with this explanation: "Last week's faculty inservice day dealt with homophobia. We began by indicating our experiences with gays and lesbians and then heard from a panel of New City School gay and lesbian parents. Our goal is to create a school in which everyone feels safe and valued and in which all of us appreciate and respect one another." I also noted the day's focus in my weekly Friday parent letter. Communicating what we are doing widens the circle by bringing more parents into the conversation.

As with so many other areas of leadership, though, we cannot judge our effectiveness on whether or not we please everyone. If we are good, then for sure we won't please everyone. This realization is captured in a continuation of a previous story. Earlier in the chapter, I talked about the meeting in which the New City School board member asked what she would see if she were in the building at midnight. "Would I know how much our school values diversity?" she asked. I shared that a rich discussion ensued and that we agreed that our physical setting needed to portray our values. I didn't share how the discussion ended, however.

After 15 to 20 minutes of that discussion, someone asked, "This conversation is great, but how will we know if we are successful?" One of my wisest board members responded, "We've just heard from a black parent who was uncomfortable with how our school looks, and it is clear that we have been remiss." He paused for emphasis. "If we are successful in making her comfortable, which we want to do, then my guess is that we will know this because some of our white families will feel that we are doing too much."

The room remained quiet as we all grappled with the insight he offered us. As in so many other complex areas, there is no solution that satisfies everyone. Trying to make everyone happy is a sure road to frustration and failure. Instead, we need to decide what is important and move forward, recognizing that any action will cause some reaction, angst, and discomfort. The job of the school leader is to constantly push forward and be prepared for the inevitable repercussions. The goal is not to avoid such feelings but to minimize them and to ensure that they occur where they are appropriate. For example, in a predominantly white school such as mine, if the goal is to help everyone be comfortable around issues of race, we need to realize that some people, those at each end of the attitude continuum, are going to be unhappy. As my board member pointed out, some whites will feel that we are doing too much; some blacks will feel that we aren't doing enough. Knowing that these tensions will exist and being willing to accept them puts us in a position to be successful.

> We need to respect others' opinions, listen to understand, and know that healthy tension builds a good team. ~Michael

Personal Commitment to Diversity

School leaders are always on display. What we do is noted, dissected, and analyzed. This scrutiny means that the big things are important, and the little things often become the big things. Do we make a point of greeting everyone with the same degree of enthusiasm? Do we chat with everyone? It is important that every parent feel known, and it is even more important that those who are in the minority feel this way. If we don't have enough time to be everywhere and greet everyone, do we make a point of ensuring that those we do talk with are not just the wealthiest or the most powerful or those who share our racial or demographic profile? When we deal with issues of diversity, do we make a point to hear all sides?

One of the characteristics that sets effective school leaders apart is their willingness to accept diversity as an issue. That means, as I've described, that they must be willing and comfortable in considering diversity—the diversity of diversities—in almost every situation. They must consciously work to see how others, others who are different in some way, might look at a situation because, in part, of that difference. School leaders must recognize that even if they believe that their school is perfect in the diversity arena (and, of course, no school is perfect in any arena), others may not see it that way, particularly those whose history rightfully causes them to be wary. It is imperative to put race on the table and for a school leader to talk openly about racial aspects of situations and how people of different races will see situations from varying perspectives. Solutions often do not come easily for issues that intersect with diversity, so it is of the utmost importance that the principal be aware of the tensions and history that can accompany them.

Because this issue is so important and because the school leader's plate is so full, one consideration is to appoint a faculty member to be a Diversity Coordinator. Without abrogating any of the principal's responsibilities, this individual can play the moral compass role, ensuring that everything at the school— from the hiring process, to the design and placement of advertisements, to the formal and informal curriculum, to the school calendar—is done with an awareness of its possible effect on diversity issues. This person could be the principal, of course, but there is something to be gained from having another faculty member live and breathe the school's diversity issues. If another person plays this role, it must be clear to everyone that the Diversity Coordinator has the ear of the principal and that her recommendations have clout.

> We spend so much time supporting students and parents that sometimes people forget that we need that support, too.
> ~Sheryl

Infusing diversity issues into our schools and diversity awareness into our leadership styles is not an option. If we are to prepare students and lead teachers, we have to spend time and energy to create a setting in which human diversity is understood and appreciated. If we fail to do this, our message is that "everyone is the same"; of course, that is ludicrous. That attitude is costly to everyone. When issues of diversity are ignored, they simply accumulate and tensions increase. By treating all people as if they are the same, we respect no one's unique contributions. Whenever we homogenize people, we all lose. If schools are to become settings in which everyone, children and adults alike, can grow, they must be places in which everyone, children and adults alike, feels safe, comfortable, respected, and appreciated.

Partnering with Parents 10

Are students' parents important? That probably seems like a silly question. Of course students' parents are important! Everyone knows that children learn best when the school and home work together. We all understand how important it is for parents to support their children's education. It is common knowledge that children benefit when their parents are involved in school.

Yet when we consider how some schools are organized, this question becomes much less silly. Offering rhetoric about the importance of involving parents in the educational enterprise is one thing; taking action to facilitate this involvement is quite another. Given that we do know how important parental involvement is to a child's success in school, it is unfortunate that there is so often a disconnect between what should be and what is.

Every school leader has an obligation to create an environment in which parents are welcome. This obligation is true of all schools and is even more true of schools in which parents are less likely to feel comfortable. Parents who were successful as students probably will be comfortable entering the school, freely asking questions and offering suggestions and criticisms. We still need to create an environment that welcomes and supports them, but this is relatively easy because they often begin with a high comfort level in school and around educators.

Sometimes parents who weren't particularly successful in school overcome this history, and they willingly interact and get involved. These parents recognize the toll that their school experiences have taken on them. Even though they may not have a high personal comfort level, they are all the more determined to ensure that their child succeeds. They are their child's advocate, working with the teacher however needed.

Other parents for whom school was difficult may have a very different attitude toward education and educators. Entering a school conjures up their personal frustrations and feelings of scholastic inadequacy, and they seem unable to overcome that history. Teachers and principals may find it harder to communicate with these parents. To be fair, some educators don't help themselves in their relationship with parents by slipping into jargon, expecting parents to sit in kid-sized chairs in meetings, and failing to communicate unless there is a problem. Irrespective of parent attitudes, we have an obligation to work with all our students' parents.

Parents are the first and best teachers of the children. ~Estella

When we encounter parents who come to school apprehensive, hesitant, or antagonistic, we have to approach them in the same way we do students: by getting to know them and working with them in an individual way that meets their needs and our own. Some parents simply require more time in a parent-teacher conference, for example. Once we know this, then we are wise not to schedule another conference immediately after theirs. (If we don't act on our knowledge, we make life harder for ourselves. The next conference invariably begins late, which means the following conference also begins late, and so on.) Some parents need to be notified *whenever* there is an issue involving their child at school; other parents assume if something is a big deal, they will be called. Some parents are at the classroom doorstep every morning; other parents need to be cajoled and reminded to attend their parent-teacher conference. Just as with children, the range of parent behaviors and responses is wide. Just as with children, our job is to work against making value judgments. Sometimes we have higher standards for our students' parents and expect them to be without fault or flaw; of course, that is just not realistic. Life is interesting precisely because none of us is perfect.

Expressing frustration about a parent's behavior is natural and appropriate: "I can't believe her mother forgot we were supposed to meet when she was the one who asked to get together!" Drawing negative inferences, however, is not appropriate, difficult as it can be to refrain from doing this. It's neither fair nor logical to follow up the frustration with comments like "She just doesn't care enough!" or "She must not think my time is important." Our job is to remember that parents are supposed to be a child's advocate, and we need to work with them to help children succeed.

Examining Institutional Habits

Recall this adage: Parents need to know that you care before they will care what you know. Do we let parents know that we understand and care about their children? If they don't know that—even if we truly do care about their children—it will affect how open and responsive they are. Do they know that we view their children as human beings, not only as learners? Do we listen? Do we practice fairness? Do we work to find the positives? These kinds of behaviors and interactions are important for any teacher or principal. If the answer to all these questions is yes, chances are that parents will be involved and supportive.

Beyond our personal interactions with parents, there can be institutional habits, practices, and policies that we follow without question. We often do so because, well, because we've always done so! Sometimes these habits are not particularly parent-friendly. For example, do our schedules for student performances and parent-teacher conferences reflect the fact that more parents today find it difficult to come to school in the middle of the day than did parents 20 years ago? As our society has become more questioning and less trusting, have we responded by sharing more information about our educational philosophy and by offering more possibilities for involvement?

The questions in Figure 12 address many of the institutional habits found in schools. These questions can help you reflect on the role of students' parents at your school and their relationships with teachers and administrators. At a minimum, it's worth asking what messages these habits give to parents.

Figure 12

Ways Schools Can Reach Out to Parents

	Never	Rarely	Sometimes	Always
1. Are teachers routinely available for ad hoc mini-conferences (before or after school)?	❑	❑	❑	❑
2. Are teachers' and administrators' phone numbers and e-mail addresses shared with parents?	❑	❑	❑	❑
3. Is there a welcoming and comfortable gathering place for parents in the school?	❑	❑	❑	❑
4. When class presentations or performances are scheduled, are evening times available to accommodate parents who work during the day?	❑	❑	❑	❑
5. Are sufficient slots for parent-teacher conferences offered during the evening to accommodate parents who work during the day?	❑	❑	❑	❑
6. Are report cards sent home prior to conferences so that parents can absorb the information before meeting?	❑	❑	❑	❑
7. Are standardized test scores sent home before parent-teacher conferences? Does a user-friendly explanation accompany the test data?	❑	❑	❑	❑
8. Do open houses or parent evenings provide sufficient time for interaction and for questions and answers?	❑	❑	❑	❑
9. Does the principal send a weekly letter to families?	❑	❑	❑	❑
10. Do classroom teachers send a weekly letter to families?	❑	❑	❑	❑
11. Do specialist teachers (art, music, physical education) regularly communicate with families?	❑	❑	❑	❑
12. Does the principal periodically solicit input and feedback from parents?	❑	❑	❑	❑

Promoting a Welcoming Attitude

I give presentations at conferences, and midway through my talk, I often say, "Now this next photo is the most important one I will share with you." The crowd—those who are still awake, anyway—leans forward in anticipation, fingers poised to write some profound words. But what is this? It's just a picture of a coffee urn sitting on a table!

Well, it's not just a coffee urn. It's the coffee urn in my school's front hall, in the parent welcoming area. Next to the urn is a sign: PARENTS, HAVE A CUP OF COFFEE; LINGER WITH US!

"This photo is of the coffee urn in our parent welcoming area, across from the office," I tell the group. "Having a parent welcoming area and offering free coffee is a statement we make about wanting parents in our school. But what I want to focus on is the phrase on the sign, *linger with us*."

I proceed to explain that not all parents drink coffee, and not all parents are in our halls in the morning. Regardless of what a parent drinks or when a parent walks by that area, the word *linger* shouts out. It says that parents are welcome in our school. The couch and chair in the parent welcoming area are inviting, and *linger* reinforces the statement we are making. The word *linger* says that not only are parents welcome here, but they don't even need a particular issue or agenda. We simply value their presence and are pleased when they hang around. (Every year, parents who are new to our school make a point of telling me how they are struck by this message and how much it pleases them.)

Other principals have gone even further in encouraging parents to come and linger in their schools. I know of one local principal who has installed a clothes washer and dryer in her building and makes it available to her students' parents at no charge. She, too, wants parents to feel comfortable about coming to the school and lingering. For her school's parent body, an opportunity to wash and dry clothes at school (instead of going

> Seek to understand before being understood. ~Barry

to the Laundromat) is effective. I cite this as a creative example of a principal who does whatever it takes to pull parents into the building. Once parents are there lingering, perhaps they can become positively involved in other ways. At a minimum, they will have an opportunity to learn about the school's educational philosophy and programs just by looking at what is on the walls. While they are there, they are able to talk to other parents, and the principal can casually chat with them, too. What the coffee pot and washer/dryer share is that they are offered specifically to encourage parents to enter the building and hang around. There are probably as many different ways to do this as there are groups of parents.

Make parents feel that they are involved, and they will help you.

~Mahmoud

I realize that encouraging this kind of parent presence opens the door to some difficulties. Yes, some parents can hang around too much and become intrusive. Yes, there are times when the "Parking Lot Mafia" can take a minor incident and magnify it beyond recognition. But the benefits of parent involvement are worth the potential price. Parents who feel welcome and invited are far more likely to become involved and supportive.

Encouraging Two-Way Communication

Two-way communication is the key to working well with parents. Sometimes we think good communication means that we are particularly eloquent, insightful, and maybe even profound. Don't get me wrong: It would be good to be eloquent, insightful, and profound. Yet these qualities alone don't necessarily constitute good communication. Good communication is two-way communication, an exchange. Just as you cannot accurately judge the quality of teaching by observing only the teacher—because it is essential to also see how students are responding and to determine what they are learning—you cannot judge the quality of communication in a school solely by the information given to parents. To effectively judge the quality of a school's communication, we must examine the opportunities for interaction between parents and teachers and between parents and school leaders. In fact, opportunities for parent-teacher interaction are generally far more common than those for parent-administrator interaction. Too often, principals hear from parents only when there is a problem.

New City School uses several specific strategies that help encourage a two-way dialogue: intake conferences, new parent coffees, and parent surveys. Each of these strategies is designed to increase parent comfort and to offer a setting in which questions or concerns can be comfortably shared. In addition, all staff members' home phone numbers and e-mail addresses are available in our school's "Buzz Book." Not unlike the word *linger*, this sends a message to parents, whether or not they ever contact a teacher.

> Remember, parents are people who lose all perspective when it comes to their children. ~Angie

Intake Conferences

At New City School, intake conferences are held during the third week of school, intentionally too early in the year for us to know much about our students. In an intake conference, parents talk and teachers listen. The expectation is that parents will talk 75 percent of the time and that teachers will listen 75 percent of the time! Before the conference, a list of possible questions is given to parents to help them think about the kinds of information they might like to share and the issues they may want to discuss.

- How does your child view school?
- What are your goals for your child this year?
- What is your child's activity schedule away from school?
- How do you deal with homework? Do you help your child with it, or do you check to make sure it's finished?
- How does your child solve problems at home?

• In which intelligences do you see your child as the strongest? Which intelligences does your child tend to avoid the most?

• In which intelligences are you, personally, the strongest? Which do you tend to avoid?

• How do you hope your child will change during this school year?

Intake conferences can also be a good time to explore diversity issues and emphasize the importance of diversity to our school. Sample questions for parents include the following:

• What holidays does your family celebrate? Will any of these family celebrations affect your child's activities at school?

• Would you share a bit about your family's heritage?

• Has your child seen family members in situations in which they were discriminated against?

• Have you talked about skin color with your child? If so, how did you approach this?

• Have you talked about economic disparities with your child? If so, how did you approach this?

• What are some of the ways that your family has worked to help your child appreciate racial, ethnic, or economic differences?

After their first intake conference at New City School, most parents don't need such lists and come with their own agenda. Beyond providing us with helpful information about students and families early in the year, the intake conference is a power equalizer. Typically, teachers—even if they have been working with a student only for a few months—are presumed to be the experts, and the job of parents is to listen. An intake conference is different. Its design reflects that parents are the experts about their children, that they have valuable insights and perceptions, and that this information will be helpful to the teacher.

New Parent Coffees

After a month of school (to give parents enough time to know what they don't know), I host several new parent coffees. Most are held in the morning at 7:45 a.m., one is held during lunch, and one or two are held at 5:00 p.m. I begin by relating an incident that happened at school or by sharing an aspect of our curriculum. "But there is really no agenda today," I say, "other than that I want to hear from you. What has surprised you, what has gone well, and what is disappointing? What would you like to know?"

I find that asking "What surprised you?" elicits far richer information than asking what has been disappointing or what people don't like. The response to the "surprise" question will sometimes contain what makes people unhappy. But because they are responding to what surprised them, they feel more comfortable—and less apprehensive—about sharing something that has made them unhappy. Even though I am fairly available and accessible, some parents are reluctant to initiate a conversation. Offering them an intimate conversational setting makes it easier for them to participate.

> It always behooves you to work well with parents, no matter how crazy they may be! ~Bonnie

Parent Surveys

What are parents thinking? How do we know this? Unless we formally solicit parents' perceptions, it is easy to think that (a) everything is wonderful and there are no problems, (b) everything is terrible and the world is coming to an end, or (c) if there is something that I should know about, I'll hear about it. The correct answer, of course, is (d) none of the above. Without reaching out and formally soliciting input, we run the risk of hearing only the acolytes and the critics. Without any data, we cannot respond to someone else who says, "I hear that a number of parents are really unhappy at your school!"

I typically send out two or three surveys per year (one after the November parent-teacher conference, one after portfolio night in the spring, and one at the end of the year). I often solicit additional feedback in a parent letter. For example, I might ask, "How is it going? I'd be interested in what adjective you would use to describe this school year." Periodically asking for parent perceptions is an important part of creating a feedback loop. (Appendix C contains a sample parent survey.)

I believe it is my job to educate parents about "best practice" in regard to what is developmentally appropriate. If I can do this with respect and compassion, parents will feel empowered and in control.

~Tamala

In addition, we work at designing our open houses so that they are more than just one-way sharing. Held during the first and second week of school (prior to the intake conference, so that parents will have some knowledge of our program), we have three open house evenings to increase the likelihood that parents of siblings can attend a session for each of their children. We begin in the school theater and then quickly move to classrooms. Teachers explain their curriculum and pedagogical approach, and they make sure to allow time for questions. We often build in reflection and interaction, with teachers guiding the dialogue: "OK, now I'd like you to turn to your neighbor, a parent of another child, and take just a couple of minutes to talk about what surprised you and what questions you might have." Many times we find that parents who have had older children in the school do a great job of interpreting and explaining.

Our open house format has changed over time. In the past, we used these evenings for parents to experience learning the same way that their children would during the school day. Parents would move from learning center to learning center or practice using several of their intelligences. The parents enjoyed the experience, and teachers felt that it was a good use of time because parents could better understand what happened at school. We began to feel that we were shortchanging the parents (and ourselves), however, because we didn't have enough time to explain our program. Consequently, we decided to move back to a more traditional model, but we still question whether we made the right decision.

Clearly, two-way communication is essential in a good school. We need to know what parents like, what concerns them, and what they question. We may not agree with what makes parents unhappy, but once we understand the issue, we can decide if there is merit in their concern and if we should respond by changing what we are doing or by improving our communication and explanations.

Making the Most of One-Way Communication

Along with two-way communication, good schools also engage in ample one-way communication (information sent from the school to parents). At my school, one-way communication primarily takes place through parent letters (though we also use the halls and walls to communicate). Each week I send home a letter to all families, and each week every classroom teacher sends home a letter to her students' parents.

> You can't support families if you are busy judging them. ~Sheryl

School leaders must take the time to inform parents about what is happening at school. Sharing not just the *what* but also the *why* enables parents to have a better understanding and appreciation of educators' efforts. I have been sending a weekly letter during each of the 28 years that I have led a school. They used to be hard-copy letters; now they are electronic, complete with photos of our students in action. (You can see my weekly letters and photos at the New City School Web site, www.newcityschool.org.) Over time, the letters have become longer and longer. In fact, occasionally I hear a complaint that my letters are too long, and I am sharing too much information. Other parents tell me that they eagerly await the letters and love the detailed explanations! My bias is to offer all the information, realizing that not everyone will read the full letter.

My letters contain important information that parents need to know: upcoming dates, sign-up procedures for sports teams, and opportunities for them to get involved. I also feature a paragraph called "Alum Success" in which I recount the achievements of our graduates as they continue their education in high school (and sometimes in college). We feature students who are on the honor roll, on a sports team, in a play or part of the stage crew, on the chess team, on student council, and so on. Because they have seen this feature in my parent letters when their children were attending my school, parents of graduates contact me to share their information. In addition, I read the high school publications to look for our graduates' successes.

I also use the letters as a tool to proselytize, to share our educational philosophy and explain what we are doing and why we are doing it. Such information is helpful not only to the parents of children in the classroom being discussed (who, I hope, already know about these topics), but also to parents of younger children. Reading what is happening allows them to peer around the corner and look into the future. Appendix D includes excerpts from two longer letters sent home last spring. (My full letters are typically three to four pages.)

They have to know that you care before they will care what you know. ~Sarah

In addition to my Friday letters, each grade level sends its own weekly letter to parents. The grade-level letter is much more focused on the activities for that particular grade: upcoming field trips, bake sales, and other special activities. Teachers also make a point of explaining an aspect of their curriculum. The combination of the two letters, mine from a schoolwide perspective and the teachers' addressing their particular grade, gives parents a rich picture of what is happening at school.

Valuing Involvement

When parents are involved in school, everyone benefits. Yet, as we all know, it is much harder to elicit parental involvement than it was even a decade ago. In my time leading schools, I have seen fewer and fewer parents with time available during the day to give us. This lack of time doesn't mean that it is impossible to get parents involved; it simply means that involvement is more difficult.

All schools have needs, from clerical help, to reading to students, to helping tutor, to tending the garden, to organizing the lost and found (which contains far more lost than found). A starting point can be to ask parents what skills and interests they have and how they would like to help. In fact, I find that the best ways to involve parents come from the discussions held at the new parent coffees. I also seek helpers in my weekly letters. As parents talk with me, a joint interest or opportunity often arises.

Strategies for parental involvement can—and should—vary by school and community. What we can do depends on the age of the students we serve, the kind of community in which we work, and the culture of the school. In every situation, though, a constant is that children learn best when their parents are supportive and involved.

School leaders must give the time and attention that is necessary to ensure that their school is a welcoming place for parents, that parents can be heard, and that parents can become involved. These goals are not easily realized, but, as with all the other aspects of school leadership, they are goals that are too important to be ignored.

11 Leading in the Year 2025

The decisions that we make today are framed by the tomorrows we envision. When we decide what type of computer operating system to buy, when we choose to hire Alice over Barry, when we determine what kinds of preparation our students need, we do so based on our assumptions about the future. Peering around the corner and predicting what will happen tomorrow, next year, or in a decade is anything but certain. Wars, stock market crashes, and last-minute umbrella sales are testament to the foolishness of feeling certain about tomorrow.

For example, in 1943, the chairman of IBM, Thomas Watson, observed, "I think there is a world market for maybe five computers." The Decca Recording Company rejected the Beatles in 1962: "We don't like their sound, and guitar music is on the way out." A 1968 edition of *Business Week* declared, "With over 50 foreign cars already on sale here, the Japanese auto industry isn't likely to carve out a big slice of the U.S. Market." (These and other "bad predictions" can be found at http://rinkworks.com/said/predictions.shtml.)

Our only certainty is that the future is uncertain. No one with any common sense would try to predict the future. Certainly no one in his or her right mind would put such thoughts in print for others to see and history to record! Those caveats aside, I will try to make a "new mistake" and look forward to the year 2025.

Let me be very clear that I disavow any special insight about the future. I didn't buy Microsoft stock, I bet on John

Kerry's victory in 2004, and I'm waiting for wide neckties to come back in style.

Though we cannot predict the future with accuracy, we can work from some logical assumptions about areas in which change is likely to take place. From there, we can speculate about what might happen in schools. Looking into my semi-cloudy crystal ball, I see three areas that will have an effect on schools and educational leadership: ever-expanding technology, changing family life, and increased accountability and competition.

Before going any further, you may want to take a few minutes and make your own forecasts about education in 2025 in these areas. How do you respond to the following questions?

1. How will technological advances affect schools?

2. How will changing family structures and demographics affect schools?

3. How will greater accountability and competition affect schools?

> A leader has to have a combination of vision and pragmatism.
>
> ~April

Ever-Expanding Technology

Trying to grasp the educational implications of technology in 2025 is so difficult because we cannot predict what technology will offer. As computer chips have become smaller, faster, and more powerful, the explosion of technology is beyond belief. The Internet was new to most of us in 1994, and e-mail was a rarity. Today, more than 888 million people use the Internet; worldwide growth has increased by 146 percent since 2000 (Internet World Stats, 2005). (At times, I feel as if all of them are sending me an e-mail message!) Today, moving, electronic images in vibrant color jump out from computer screens, and personal digital assistants contain libraries full of information that can be carried around in a coat pocket. Running shoes with computer chips implanted in the soles monitor a runner's speed and distance.

Technology is everywhere, but this is just the beginning. In *The Age of Spiritual Machines*, Ray Kurzweil (1999) paints a future in which the differences between humans and computers will become blurred. Kurzweil predicts that by the year 2019

• A $1,000 personal computer will be approximately equal to the computational ability of the human brain.

• Computers will be so small that they will be virtually invisible, and they will be everywhere—embedded in walls, tables, clothing, jewelry, and human bodies.

• Paper books or documents will be rare, and most instruction will be done by simulated, software-based teachers.

Further, in *Are We Spiritual Machines?* (2002), Kurzweil predicts that "by the second half of this . . . century, there will be no distinction between human and machine intelligence" (p. 55). Rodney Brooks (2002) expands the role of technology: "It seems reasonable to assume that by the year 2050 we will be able to intervene and select not just the sex of a baby at the point of conception but also many of its physical, mental, and personality characteristics as well, a much less trivial matter" (p. 190).

If we assume that Kurzweil and Brooks are correct (or even if they are only one-third right), the implications for school leaders are profound. First, school leaders will have to be comfortable with technology, *very* comfortable. This comfort will be important so that they can use technology to help them lead and also so that they can model its use for others. Technological advances will cause schools to gather, massage, monitor, and report new and different kinds of student achievement and growth data; principals will have to be adept in doing this.

A high comfort level with technology will also be important so that school leaders will know when the use of technology is *not* appropriate. Without taking anything away from the potential of technology to foster student learning or to help leaders in running schools, technology can be overused and used improperly. In *The Flickering Mind* (2003), Todd Oppenheimer recounts

> Schools require fewer chief organizers and more courageous disorganizers. Those who hear and hold up great ideas and visions also see strengths of others as the fastest way to genius innovations at school.
>
> ~Ellen

tale after tale of how educators gravitated to technological solutions without understanding the technology or appreciating what it could and could not do. As with any other tool, before we use a technological device, we need to ask if it is the right solution for the problem we are trying to solve.

Another implication of continued technological advances is that the school building or campus will no longer be the only, or perhaps the primary, location in which formal learning takes place. Indeed, this trend has already begun at the university and professional development levels. The University of Phoenix, primarily offering online courses, enrolls more than 200,000 students at 150 centers in the United States (Read, 2005). Many other colleges and universities also offer online courses (as does ASCD). Sometimes the online courses are purely electronic; at other times, they offer a hybrid approach that includes some face-to-face interactions.

Soon we will see secondary schools routinely offering online courses. Beyond the obvious advantage of allowing students to work at their own pace and appealing to those who do not want a full school experience, electronic learning will allow students to hold paying jobs at times other than in the afternoon and evening. What this means, of course, is that fewer teachers will be in schools between 8:00 a.m. and 4:00 p.m. The Internet—or its successor (three-dimensional, full-size, submersion video?)—will also be used in supervising these teachers. Perhaps the Internet will be used in supervising most teachers.

Though online classes will become more and more popular, I find it hard to imagine online teaching playing a significant role when students are under 10 or 12 years of age. Younger students need a relationship with a teacher and require more direction; not insignificantly, they are also less able to be home alone without supervision. Yet the potential of the Internet cannot be overestimated. The Internet will give every teacher the opportunity to teach every child. A teacher in Omaha, Nebraska, will be able to share her passion and expertise simultaneously with students across the country and around the world. They will hear, see, and interact with her as if she were 5 or 10 feet from them. Indeed, Ray Kurzweil would probably say that for all practical purposes, she *will* be 5 or 10 feet from the students; they won't know whether she is in the room with them or in Omaha or Singapore. The notion of "online" learning may be replaced by "on touch" learning, with students able to touch and handle technologically created images—to shake the hand of the teacher from Singapore or to touch the scarf that she wears.

You may be thinking, *I've heard these kinds of claims before.* After all, similar predictions were made for instruction on educational television 40 years ago. I know from firsthand experience. Back then, I sat in a high school English class that was taught by someone who was somewhere else. My classmates and I found it very easy to ignore the lectures that emanated from the talking face on the 15-inch, black-and-white screen in the front of our classroom. We never met or talked with the teacher, so he remained a distant, two-dimensional person who was no larger than a foot tall. Our interactions were limited to sending him letters through the mail and listening to him read some of them on the air more than a week later. In contrast, tomorrow's technology will be fully interactive, so the term *interactive* will lose its meaning. *Interactive* will hearken back to an earlier time, and people will find the word hard to fathom (perhaps like the words *icebox* or *liquid paper* are today). Technology of the future will also be less visible, if not invisible. (This change is already happening. We are largely unaware of the fact that more of the cost of a new car is due to the computers embedded in the automobile than for the steel used in its chassis.)

Advances in technology will change how we communicate with students' parents. Communication to and from the home will be easier, quicker, more encompassing—capturing more aspects of a student's growth—and more frequent. Already, some parents can visit a Web site to see how their child did in school today (and ascertain that their student *was* in school!).

When parents and teachers have access to the same information, many of the tensions that arise from parents seeing their child one way and teachers viewing her another will disappear. As a result, parents and teachers will become closer partners in education. This same technology will also change—has already changed—how we communicate in organizations. E-mail makes it easy and acceptable for virtually any employee to contact any other employee, regardless of geographical distance or organizational position.

What does all this mean for school leaders? Paradoxically, I believe that the increased pervasiveness of and reliance on technology will make the human touch even more important. If for no other reason, face-to-face interactions and relationships will carry greater weight because there will be fewer of them. With apologies to Mr. Kurzweil, I have to believe that no computer program will be able to supplant the interactions between human beings. However, because computers will offer a reasonable facsimile and because, as I have suggested, we will rely on them more and more, the special human touch will, literally and figuratively, be essential. Regardless of what technology offers and the shape of future communications, good schools will still be collegial settings in which adults grow and learn together. Tomorrow's principals will find ways to use technology to promote that collegiality while preserving the important role of face-to-face interactions.

> Don't expect me to step up to the plate if I feel I'm already doing too much. ~Bonnie

Changing Family Life

Families have changed, with children often suffering as a result. The nuclear family, consisting of a mother, a father, and their biological or adoptive descendants, is in decline. The divorce rate appears to have leveled off, but too many marriages still end in divorce. A significant number of children live in poverty and come to school with unmet physical and emotional needs. Millions of children are without adequate health care, and, in some settings, their physical safety cannot be guaranteed. Unfortunately, looking ahead, there is nothing to suggest that these conditions will improve considerably. Such changes do not, however, abrogate the responsibilities of educators. We take each child as he walks through our doors and do everything we can to help him learn.

These conditions suggest that the trend for schools to assume responsibilities for the noninstructional aspects of a child's well-being and growth will continue and even accelerate. We will see more integration of community services, and many of these services will be housed within the school. In fact, some school principals are already doing this. A good example is the principal who has installed a clothes washer and dryer for her students' parents to use (discussed in Chapter 10).

The possibilities of what schools might do to support families are virtually unlimited. As the disparity between the needs of children and the ability of families to meet those needs increases, more and more responsibilities will fall to schools and be assigned to or taken on by principals. Years ago, for example, in trying to figure out ways to support our New City School parents, we considered offering a dry-cleaning service. We contemplated housing a bin into which parents could drop their dirty clothes in the morning. At mid-morning, the cleaners would collect the clothing. They would return the clean clothes to school the following day to be collected by parents when they came to pick up their children. Wiser heads prevailed (I think), and we decided that we didn't want a bin of dirty clothing in our front hall. Also, I remember thinking that if a parent was displeased with the amount of starch in the shirts, you-know-who—not the cleaners!—would receive the brunt of parental displeasure. Though it seemed ludicrous that parents would be unhappy with me about starch in their shirts, I recognize the merit in this logic. After all, if we are going to provide or house a service, even if it is cleaning clothes, we should have some responsibility for its quality. (Looking ahead, I figure that once we finally

> The administrator has to understand and respect the dynamics of being a classroom teacher. ~Tamala

do bite the bullet and offer a laundry service, we'll place student art on the sides of the bin to make it more attractive, or maybe we'll use that space to remind parents about the upcoming vision screening, voter registration, or administration of flu shots.)

Inevitably, the many roles of school leaders will become more encompassing and complex. Instead of "simply" being responsible for students' educational progress, school leaders will be in charge of other activities, from serving breakfast and lunch (as is already the case in many schools), to offering after-school programming, to providing space for dental and health services, to housing infant care and babysitting, to including senior citizens in activities, to opening schools during the evenings and on weekends to address other social and family needs.

As mind-boggling as this explosion of services may sound, elements of it are already happening. At New City School, our classes start at 8:30 a.m. and end at 3:30 p.m. However, we offer free care beginning at 7:00 a.m. and provide extended day services, for a fee, until 6:30 p.m. Our extended day program provides a study hall, access to our computer lab, and time for students to play games and have fun in a low-key yet supervised way. The extended day program also offers talents classes (chess, art, music, newspaper) for a fee. Each day more than half of our students remain after school in the extended day program. We also provide camps and supervision during spring break, winter break, summer vacation, and on the days that school is closed for parent-teacher conferences and inservice sessions.

Like many other schools, we constantly look for new ways to support our families. As I write, we are converting one of our two gymnasiums into a 5,400-square-foot multiple intelligences library. It will include a mezzanine, lots of nooks and crannies, a mini-theater, a wealth of books, and many ways for children to learn and show what they know. But that is not enough. We are planning to widen the scope of the library's uses and users as another way to support families. The library will be available after school, from 3:30 to 6:00 p.m., for parents who want to read to or work with their children and for parents who have one child with them while they wait for another to finish soccer, basketball, or softball practice (all of which are held at school). We are planning to open our school on a Saturday morning each month to enable neighbors to use the library (even though a new public library is within a mile of our school). Discussions are also taking place about capitalizing on our new space by holding an evening speakers series in which educators would come to our school to talk to parents and community members. Finally, the library will include an area that is designed to encourage parents to have a cup of coffee and linger. (As described in Chapter 10, there is already a parent area in the alcove in the main hall across from my office, and parents frequently linger there throughout the day. A second area is needed because we have more lingerers than space.) The new library will not only embrace our students, but it will also be a vehicle for us to reach out to the community.

As the scope of services provided by schools expands, the resources that are needed and the connections that must be made will increase exponentially. Principals, already lacking time to do all that is needed to lead their schools, will find themselves responsible for more outside activities and external relationships. The danger, of course, is that a principal will be responsible for so many varied tasks, she will not be able to succeed with any of them. As the scope of responsibilities expands, I envision schools using administrative aides to assist principals in these nonscholastic arenas. (The funding for these positions will likely come from sources other than the school district's budget.) These individuals, probably without a degree in education and perhaps without any university degree at all, would serve the role of community broker: identifying resources, developing relationships, planning programs, and overseeing their operation. Of course, this role could also serve as a training position for administrative interns or aspiring principals.

As another strategy to reach out into the community, many schools will form neighborhood advisory boards. These boards will be composed primarily of people who do not have a child attending the school (although some members may be parents of alumni). Board members will work with principals in two areas: pushing services out of the school and into the community and pulling resources into the school from the community. Principals will find working with such groups a different sort of challenge than working with faculty or parents. Because the purview of the neighborhood advisory boards will go far beyond the educational realm (and may not even include it), principals will need to develop new interests and areas of expertise. This will probably require principals to play an even more political and facilitative role, as they continually balance competing interests while searching for the common good.

This trend means that, as we have begun to see with superintendent selection, principals will be more likely to come to the job from noneducational backgrounds and with different kinds of preparation and training. Although there will always be opportunities for traditional educators to run schools—teachers who become administrators and hold a master's or doctoral degree in administration—the focus in selecting leaders will be more on the skills candidates possess and less on their teaching experience or academic preparation. As the role of the school expands and changes, social workers or counselors may have an appropriate skill set for leading schools. A director of development may be great at building the relationships, or an attorney might excel at planning the strategies, that are necessary to run a school. Someone with a background in marketing might be the ideal person to inspire a staff and coalesce a community. Some school leaders may possess these abilities, and it is possible, of course, that these skills could be found on the school's neighborhood advisory board. One thing seems clear, however: Regardless of the presence of administrative aides or advisory boards, tomorrow's principals will need to be knowledgeable

> Strong administrators are not afraid to roll up their sleeves and work.
> ~Kathy

about issues outside of education and skillful in dealing with a wide range of people, not only parents.

Increased Accountability and Competition

Leading a school will be even more challenging in the future than it is today; given today's realities, that is saying something! Two distinct movements are coming together to heighten accountability and the competitive environment of schools. These movements are (1) an increasing use of quantitative analysis in judging schools and (2) greater school choice for parents.

By *quantitative analysis*, I mean that we—educators, parents, politicians, and members of the media—increasingly count, measure, and then compare. The No Child Left Behind Act is the avatar of this quantitative, high-stakes movement, but it by no means stands alone. The testing industry is flourishing as we compare our students' progress to that of their classmates, to that of students around the United States, and to that of students living in other parts of the world. When we rely on numbers to ascertain value (whether the numbers are percentages, percentiles, grade-equivalents, or stanines), comparisons are easy and inevitable. As data are made more public, we will find schools being held more accountable for students' performances on these tests. This reliance on hard data is not necessarily a bad thing. We should know how our students are achieving, and we should use data to monitor, plan, and evaluate. Nonetheless, the ease of comparison increases the likelihood of comparison. More and more, school leaders will be held accountable for student performance.

Some argue (I am among them) that quantitative analyses typically overlook much of what contributes to a quality education and prepares students to succeed in the real world. How can we use a number to indicate a student's appreciation of aesthetics, kindness to animals, or concern for others? How can we

use a number to measure a student's motivation when confronted by adversity, sense of humor when everything goes
wrong, or creativity and resourcefulness when dealing with
changing complexities? To me, these gaps point out the major
shortcoming in a reliance on quantitative data. Too often, we
measure what is measurable and ignore what is valuable.

However, as I look to the future, I have no doubt that psycho-
metric and technological advances will make it possible to
record and track students' attitudes and values. We can (and
will) question the validity of such instruments, but they will
become prevalent. Testing companies will respond as schools
seek wider and richer ways to document student growth. On the
one hand, this will be an improvement because we will be able to
determine, for example, the empathy of our students and know
whether their concern for others has increased over time. On the
other hand, as these qualities and attributes become measurable,
they will be counted and compared. Cyber-newspapers in the year
2025 (by then, *newspaper*, too, may be an obsolete term, along
with *liquid paper*) will not only rank schools on their students'
reading comprehension and mathematical calculation skills; they
also will compare schools on their students' performance on
standardized measures of empathy, creativity, and tenacity.

> A good leader has the power to make the people he or she works with look good.
>
> ~Debbie

The other factor that will accelerate the movement toward
greater accountability is greater parent choice. Indeed, this shift
is already taking place. According to Hassel and Hassel (2004),
"Fully 12.5 million children attended schools other than their
assigned public schools in 2003 (not including home-schooled
children), up from just 8.6 million in 1993, an increase of 45 percent" (p. 34). Charter schools have played a role in this phenomenon. They offer an alternative to the local public school, and
they raise the issue of choice in the educational arena. The first
charter school legislation was passed in the early 1990s, and
there are already more charter schools (3,000) than independent
schools in the United States. Although these schools are not
without problems and challenges, the genie named "charter

schools" cannot be placed back in its bottle. Invariably, more and more charter schools will be created each year. The educational merit of charter schools aside (and I do believe they have merit), their presence is a manifestation of the consumer movement that we see in practically every other sector of society. Compared to 20 years ago, today's U.S. consumers have far more choices in food, clothing, automobiles, and television programs. There is no reason to think that this trend will be different in the educational arena. When for-profit and "e-schools" are added to the mix of options available to parents, education, whether we like it or not, will become another commodity.

It is essential to offer opportunities in which a staff can cooperate, brainstorm ideas and solutions, reflect and give feedback. ~Sande

Public school districts will respond to the competition by offering more options among and within their schools. Rather than striving to create cookie-cutter schools with identical offerings throughout the geographical areas that they serve (however good the cookie being cut), public schools will begin to create unique identities and fashion themselves around curricular thrusts. When a district has multiple elementary schools, why not frame one around a basics curriculum, another around the arts, and a third around the outdoors? Parents could select from among the options within their district. Likewise, if there are several high schools, why not devote one to the arts and another to the sciences? Years ago, of course, this was done when magnet schools were created as tools to facilitate racial desegregation.

The benefits of giving consumers and staff members a choice are extraordinary. When parents are able to choose the curriculum and context for their children, cognitive dissonance becomes a factor and they and their children begin the experience with a higher degree of loyalty. This means future principals will need to have marketing expertise, too. Of course, this doesn't necessarily mean that the principal must personally possess marketing expertise. At a minimum, though, the principal must be able to draw upon the marketing expertise of others. Marketing has already been given a good deal of attention at my school. An independent school, we must market ourselves to prospective parents. But that is not enough. Because we have a unique educational philosophy—valuing academics, student diversity, multiple intelligences, thematic instruction, and the personal intelligences—that is vastly different from that of the schools many of our students' parents attended, we need to market ourselves to them as well. We need our current students' parents to understand what we do and why we do it; we need them to appreciate the values of our school and the value of enrolling and re-enrolling their child with us. This is why we use the halls not just to decorate, but also to educate. It is why we put such emphasis on encouraging our parents to enter the building and linger with us. It is the reason why I expend considerable efforts on parent education and communication. When we maintain good communication with our consumers (our students) and our customers (their parents), everyone benefits.

Leaders and Distributed Intelligence

If I am correct in my hunches about the future, then the jobs of school leaders will become even more complex and challenging. More and wider responsibilities will be placed on the principal's plate. As a result, principals will have to develop different skills and invest more hours if they are to succeed. This scenario does not portend well for the future of principals or schools. Most principals will say that they already spend too much time on their jobs, yet they still feel frustrated at not being able to do enough or to do it well enough. These tensions can be seen in Figure 5 (p. 89). School districts already have difficulty finding enough good principals, and increased demands and expectations will make it even harder to find and keep good principals.

The solution to this daunting scenario lies in how principals define their roles. Principals need to recognize that their job is to create a school culture in which everyone grows and learns, including themselves. They must see themselves as team members and recognize that they can be smarter because of the people around them. The notion of *distributed intelligence* is relevant to this interactive definition of leadership, and distributed intelligence will be integral to the success of tomorrow's principals. Distributed intelligence is the recognition that our intelligence is not limited to what is inside our skin; our intelligence is determined, in part, by our ability to identify and use the resources around us. (The term *distributed intelligence* was initially used to refer to the increased power generated when a series of computers were linked together. Salomon's 1993 book, *Distributed Cognitions*, offers much food for thought about distributed intelligence.)

When we solve real-world problems by relying upon calculators, computers, books, artifacts, or the people around us, we are using our distributed intelligence. Mentally calculating the problem 4 x 312 uses our logical-mathematical intelligence, but solving 4 x 312 with a calculator uses distributed intelligence. (For that matter, if one needed to use a calculator to compute 2 + 2, that would be using distributed intelligence.) Solving a navigation problem by gazing at the stars is using spatial intelligence; doing so with a global positioning satellite device or some other tool is using distributed intelligence. If two people have access to a library to solve a problem, but only one knows the Dewey Decimal System, her distributed intelligence will enable her to be more effective in identifying and accessing the library resources. Smart people have always used their distributed intelligence, whether inferring from symbols written on a cave wall, predicting the weather from a cloud formation, or choosing teammates who will make the team stronger.

It is tempting to think of distributed intelligence primarily as an ability to use technology. Technology is everywhere, it seems, and those who can use technology do have an advantage over those who cannot. This was true in the 1450s when Johannes Gutenberg invented a method of printing from moveable type, and it is even more true today. Indeed, knowing how to effectively access technology—knowing what technology is relevant and will help solve the problem—is using distributed intelligence. Capitalizing on technology is only part of distributed intelligence, but, to me, it is the least important aspect.

In my mind, the best use of a leader's distributed intelligence is manifested in her ability to draw from the people around her. Leaders with a strong distributed intelligence will recognize the strengths of others and see how they can use, work with, and learn from these strengths. They will know their own weaknesses and look to buttress them through complementary relationships. For example, a leader with a strong distributed intelligence will be able to make great use of the neighborhood advisory board described earlier in this chapter. She will know the areas in which she is weak (perhaps marketing, facilities, or finances), and she will find individuals who have these skills so that she can learn from them and encourage them to use their talents to assist her in solving problems. Even without an advisory board, a leader with a strong distributed intelligence will have a sense for the strengths possessed by others and how they can fit with, or support, her own profile. A strong leader seeks others with whom she can work well and from whom she can learn.

As I noted at the beginning of this chapter, peering into the future is no easy task. Looking ahead, it is clear that the only constant will be change. We know that society will change and that schools will be required to change and evolve in response. But we also know that regardless of how schools are asked to change, strong leadership will be essential if teachers and students are to succeed. Strong leaders create a setting in which everyone learns and grows.

> Leaders can be consumers or releasers of energy. Good leadership is about being able to unlock employee energy. ~Janice

Afterword

First, assuming you're reading this after you've read all the other words in this book, thank you for your interest and your patience. I hope that what I have written will be helpful to you, regardless of your position or context. Despite the myriad of suggestions and "how to" strategies that I offer, I believe my role is to raise more questions and offer fewer answers.

Writing this book has been a humbling experience. Reflecting on various topics has repeatedly reminded me of what I don't do as often, or as quickly, or as well as I should. It has also reminded me of what I do too often, too slowly, and not well enough. I write with no false modesty; I do many things well and a few things quite well. But writing this book has graphically reminded me of where I fall short of my expectations. Like my Saturday morning basketball games, writing this book has brought me face to face with the disparity between hope and reality.

Self-flagellation aside, writing this book has been extraordinarily good for me. I have read widely, examined others' strategies and practices, examined my own leadership style, and reflected on what I should be doing differently. I've engaged in wonderfully rich e-mail conversations and debates with many people, the majority of whom I've not met in person. Although I'm always looking at what we and I don't do well at New City School, writing this book has enabled me—no, *caused* me—to look at everything we do. The axiom "If it ain't broke, don't fix it" becomes "Break it so that it can be fixed to be better than before." Already, we have completely changed our professional goal-setting process at New City School. I've also thought quite differently about how to run meetings and draw in members of our community. I have had some wonderful discussions about human diversity, teacher creativity, teacher evaluation, and the need to focus everyone's energies. Realistically, a lot of this would not have happened without my writing. I hope that reading this book causes you to step back and question, debate, re-examine, and hypothesize in your own school setting.

Always Learning

As I reread what I have written, I hope that I have not presented too daunting a picture of running a school. Chapter after chapter recounts problems, after all. Because my intent is to offer strategies and solutions and to raise questions, I've necessarily focused on the difficulties and challenges. Of course, there is far more to running a school than the difficulties, pervasive and overwhelming as they can sometimes be.

> Life is a series of new beginnings. Leap and the net will appear.
> ~Debbie

One of the best parts of the job, for me anyway, is that despite the cyclical nature of the school calendar and the many predictable aspects of the job, the work is never dull. Every day offers routines, but each day also offers something new and something different. Even as our children and our staff members stay the same, they change; they grow older, and they develop. The aging process, last I looked, is beyond our purview, but school leaders can have a powerful influence on how students and teachers develop.

It is a given that the principal can have a powerful influence on student achievement, however that is measured. The principal does this with her team, by working with the school's faculty. When students excel, it is because everyone has grown and learned. Good principals set a tone of growth; good principals also grow, and they enthusiastically share their growth, along with their challenges, with their staff members. Helping everyone develop is the school leader's main responsibility. All that she does should lead to growth and development. How could this be anything but exciting?

Making a Difference

Last year, just before our graduation ceremony, a father whose youngest child was about to graduate asked to see me for a moment. The audience was settled in, the flowers were on the stage, and our soon-to-be graduates were lining up in the hall. My immediate thought was, *Uh-oh, what is the problem?*

The father pulled me aside, grabbed my hand, and put his arm on my shoulder. "Thank you for being here for all my children," he said. He then talked briefly about what sort of men his boys were becoming and how I had played a role in their lives.

I was, for once, speechless. I hugged him, took a deep breath, thanked him for his confidence, and thanked him for sharing his family with us. All our graduation ceremonies are significant and emotional, but because of what he said, this one was even more special. In the months since that time, I've thought a lot about that moment and also about all the students and staff members with whom I've come in contact over the years.

In *Managing the Nonprofit Organization*, Peter Drucker (1992) observes that those of us who work in nonprofit organizations have a special responsibility. The question that can be asked, that *should* be asked, when we are gone from this world is, "Have we made it a better place?" Through our actions—through the policy decisions, the day-to-day strategies, the difficult meetings, the individual conferences, the standards we hold, the flexibility we offer, the support we provide, the tenacity we show, the creativity we contribute, the smiles we give and elicit, and the doughnuts we bring—have we made a positive difference?

The differences we make may not be momentous or, even, obvious. Occasionally, our actions and roles are visible. In many cases, however, our true work will be known only by us and a few others. In some cases, we, alone, will know the role we

> Always remember to keep a good sense of humor. ~Laurie

played. Leading a school is not about recognition and fame; it is about making a difference in both big and little ways. Both of these are important. Little differences accumulate, and little differences change trajectory; little differences often result in big changes.

The opportunity to make a difference for children, to touch the future through them, has never been more exciting—or more needed—than it is today. Society expects more and offers less. For many children, children from all socioeconomic levels and backgrounds, schools remain the pathway to a better tomorrow. Archimedes purportedly said, "Give me a lever long enough and a fulcrum on which to place it, and I shall move the world." School leaders understand that statement; we do this each and every day. We lead and give direction, but that is not all. We simultaneously challenge and support. We set a tone in which individuals are valued. We create an environment that encourages risk taking and growth. We hold high expectations, and we support everyone's efforts.

Ending at the Beginning

Effective leaders begin by knowing their talents and challenges. They understand how their leadership skills relate to problems, and they use their distributed intelligence in identifying and surrounding themselves with individuals whose skills and talents will make them stronger. They know that leadership is not just due to what the leader possesses; leadership is not just about their vision, intellect, and skills. Like teaching, leadership is an art. Effective leadership is characterized by the leader's ability to make others better, to help them to grow, to support and challenge them, and to learn from and with them. Thus, we end where we began: *Leadership is about relationships.*

Appendixes

New City School
Teaching Application

NEW CITY SCHOOL
5209 Waterman Avenue • St. Louis, MO 63108 • 314-361-6411

New City School is an urban independent school that provides children from preschool through 6th grade with a challenging, individualized education in a joyful and creative environment. We seek to develop caring, confident, lifelong learners through academics, ambience, and diversity.

Application for Teaching Position
(please print)

Date of Application _____

Pre-K   K   1   2   3   4   5   6
Circle GRADE LEVEL(S) preferred

Name _____
　　　　Last　　　　　　　　　　　　　　　First　　　　　　　　　　　　　　M.I.

Address _____

Home Phone _____ Daytime Phone_____ E-mail Address _____

Social Security No. _____ Ethnic Background (optional) _____

How did you hear of New City School?_____

Have you ever been convicted of a misdemeanor or felony, other than a routine traffic violation?
___ Yes ___ No   If Yes, please explain. _____

Have you ever been the subject of a child abuse or child neglect investigation? ___ Yes ___ No
If Yes, please explain. _____

(Applicants who are offered a position will be required to complete a screening form that is sent to the Missouri Division of Family Services before employment is finalized.)

Use this space as you wish, as another way to tell us, or show us, something about you. Let yourself go. Be creative. Be humorous. Be adventurous. Be serious. You decide.

INSTRUCTIONS: Please complete this application in full and mail it to Personnel, New City School, at the above address. Also include a copy of your current résumé, including references.

We will not be able to interview everyone who applies. You will be notified if you are selected to be interviewed.

Please answer the following questions **in your own handwriting.** If necessary, attach additional sheets.

1. Are there differences between success in school and success in life?

2. Describe, as developmentally appropriate for the age of students that you would like to teach, what issues of human diversity are important and how they should be addressed.

3. What book or work of art has had the greatest impact on you?

I certify that the information provided by me in this application is true and complete.

_____

Applicant's Signature

We appreciate your interest in New City School. Thank you for applying for a teaching position with us.

New City School Performance Pay Plan

Purpose

The New City School (NCS) merit pay plan, originally adopted in 1984, is designed to attract and keep the best teachers at NCS. We recognize that a school is only as good as the quality of its teachers, no better and no worse. To that end, teacher observations, reflection, and collegiality are engendered and supported to help develop the best teachers possible.

Process

Criteria

At the end of each year, teachers are evaluated on five components of effective teaching:

1. knowledge of subject matter
2. knowledge of child development and the learning process
3. presentation skills
4. student rapport and enthusiasm
5. professionalism and collegiality

These evaluations are based on formal and informal observations, as well as other data. The categories *below average, average, superior, outstanding,* and *excellent* constitute the rating scale.

In order to remain employed at New City School, a teacher must be rated in one of the three categories above *average* (*superior, outstanding,* or *excellent*) in all five components by the end of the third year. *Average* ratings are not acceptable after three years. Further, if a teacher is *below average* in any one component in any year, the administration may elect not to offer that teacher a contract for the following year.

Professional Growth Conferences

Each teacher has a goal-setting professional growth conference (PGC) with a member of the administration in the fall. Typically, teachers frame their goals to address specific issues or themes. In some years, for example, goals were generated for academics, ambience, or diversity. In other years, goals focused on linguistics, multiple intelligences (MI), diversity, or teaming. The teacher and administrator also meet mid-year for a goal-focused PGC, at which time progress toward the goal or a change in strategies is discussed. A final goal-focused PGC is held in April or May. At this meeting, the teacher and administrator review the teacher's progress and talk about how to capitalize on this effort during the next school year. An additional PGC conference is held in the late spring or early summer, during which the administrator gives the teacher the annual evaluation and contract for the following year.

Each teaching team also develops a team goal. This goal is framed around a schoolwide issue, such as increasing parent communications or supporting diversity efforts. The goal is submitted on one sheet and is signed by all team members. Team progress toward this goal is discussed with the team at the end of the year.

Observations

Teachers who are new to NCS will be formally observed by an administrator at least six times per year. Administrators observe in the classroom, take notes, and give the teacher a write-up of the lesson. The write-up contains both observation notes (what was happening) and evaluative comments (what

worked, what was unsuccessful, what could have been done differently). Often in the summary of the lesson, the administrator
will note a teacher's efforts in a particular evaluative component
(such as knowledge of subject matter or child development and
the learning process).

After reaching a rating of *superior* or better on all five evaluation components, the number of formal observations a teacher
receives may decrease to three per year or less (although formal
or informal observations may be done at any time at the discre-
tion of the administration). Teachers and administrators may
also fashion a plan that enables teachers to use peer observations or conferences, videotaped lessons and analysis, or portfolios to document their progress.

Salary Increases

Each year, the New City School Board of Directors grants an
amount of money for salary increases, and the administration
determines the formula for distributing the raises, that is, how
much is allocated to cost-of-living increases, which are distributed to all teachers, and how much is allocated to merit
increases, which are earned by individual teachers. Individual
salary increases are a function of these two factors: a cost-of-
living adjustment and a merit raise. The dollar value of a merit
point is determined by the amount available for merit raises and
the total number of points achieved by the faculty. An individual's merit raise is determined by both these figures and, most
significant, by how the teacher is rated in each of the five
components. A rating of *average* or *below average* in a category
does not yield any merit points; merit points and merit
increases are given only for ratings of *superior, outstanding,*
and *excellent.*

Review Committee

A board Review Committee may be formed to meet with any
teacher who feels that he or she has been treated unfairly in

these areas. The committee will provide a hearing and meet with the school leader afterward. The committee does not have the authority to overturn the decision of the administration but will share information with the board's executive or evaluation committees as appropriate.

Components of Teacher Evaluation

Knowledge of Subject Matter

The teacher is knowledgeable about the topics, issues, and skills being taught; the teacher is able to relate to and use other relevant information. The teacher

• understands material sufficiently to give clear and accurate directions and to answer questions correctly;
• understands the interrelationships of content areas and can integrate subject matter into other areas of the curriculum;
• applies subject matter to current situations that occur in and out of school;
• is knowledgeable about the theory of MI;
• directs students to appropriate resources; and
• infuses diversity into lessons on a regular basis.

Knowledge of Child Development and the Learning Process

The teacher understands the principles of how children learn constructively and developmentally; the teacher individualizes instruction, uses small groups, and incorporates MI to meet each child's needs. The teacher

• uses a variety of teaching styles (including different materials and varying lesson lengths) in consideration of student learning styles and abilities;
• addresses student needs and interests on an individual basis;

- understands how each child uses a variety of intelligences to learn;
- develops lesson plans that stem, where possible, from student interests as well as student demographic characteristics, particularly racial and socioeconomic characteristics;
- frequently assesses and monitors student progress; and
- assesses while teaching to make appropriate modifications.

Presentation Skills

The teacher uses a variety of techniques in presenting instruction and facilitating learning; the teacher incorporates MI throughout instruction and assessment. The teacher

- uses a variety of teaching strategies;
- employs a variety of intelligences in instruction and assessment;
- asks stimulating, open-ended, higher-level thinking questions, as well as appropriate closed-ended, factual questions;
- plans so that the length of a lesson is appropriate to the ages and attention spans of the children; and
- presents so that students are active, rather than passive, learners.

Student Rapport and Enthusiasm

The teacher and the students genuinely like, enjoy, and respect one another. The teacher

- is an enthusiastic teacher and an enthusiastic learner;
- maintains discipline and classroom control;
- elicits the students' desire to learn;
- demonstrates and fosters a sense of respect for each child; and
- encourages students to respect one another.

Professionalism and Collegiality

The teacher deals with other adults in a professional manner; the teacher learns with and from colleagues. The teacher

- establishes good communication with parents;
- establishes good communication with peers;
- establishes good communication with administrators;
- accepts criticism and works to improve deficiencies;
- actively participates in committee work; and
- engages in reflective practice.

Credit for identifying many of the behaviors in this list goes to Patricia Nuernberger, Assistant Head for Academics, New City School.

Spring Parent Survey

May 2004

Dear Parents,

Children learn best when the school and home work together! And an important part of that working together is **two-way** communication. As you know by now, we communicate a great deal *to* you: You receive weekly letters from your child's teachers and from me, and there are newsletters and annual reports along with other mailings. In addition, our halls and walls abound with samples of student work and information.

But as good as this is, it is **one-way** communication, communication from us to you. For our children to learn best, for us to improve, I need to hear from you. **I need to know your thoughts on what you value most at New City School and in what areas you think we need to improve.**

Your thoughts are important. Even if you have done this once or 10 times before, please take 10 minutes to give me your feedback. This survey is being mailed and attached to the Friday e-letter.

To facilitate your response, I have enclosed a stamped, self-addressed return envelope. Please complete and return this survey by **June 1.** If you have more than one child at New City School, please return a different survey for each child (or indicate the various grade levels of your children on the one survey that you do return, ideally filling out the survey in a different color of ink for each child). And please indicate if you would like a personal response from me. In advance, thanks. I look forward to hearing from you.

Sincerely,

Thomas R. Hoerr, PhD
Head of School
trhoerr@newcityschool.org

P.S. If you wish, e-mail me your responses!

SPRING 2004 PARENT SURVEY
Please return by **June 1.**

Name (optional) _____

E-mail (please print) _____

Check here _____ **if you would like a personal response from me** (but if you check here, you need to provide your name or I cannot contact you!).

Please circle your child's grade level:
Pre-K   K   1   2   3   4   5   6

Including this year, indicate the number of years that your child has been enrolled:
1   2   3   4   5   6   7   8   9   10   11   12

1. **Why did you select New City School (NCS) for your child?** Please rank the reasons; #1 = most important.

   a. Strong academic program. _____

   b. Focus on the personal intelligences and nurturing environment. _____

   c. Family support program. _____

   d. Value of racial and socioeconomic diversity. _____

   e. NCS location. _____

   f. Use of multiple intelligences. _____

   g. Lower cost than most other independent schools. _____

   h. Are there other factors that are not listed? If so, please list and prioritize them:

   _____   _____

   _____   _____

2. **Which of the factors listed in Question 1 are essential to your child's being here?** Please go back and place an asterisk (*) by any factors that you consider essential in choosing NCS.

3. Please give three words that describe NCS' **strengths:**

4. Please give three words that describe NCS' **weaknesses:**

For questions 5–7, please check off the response that most closely captures your feelings. Narrative comments and clarifications are always welcome.

	Strongly Agree	Agree	Disagree	Strongly Disagree
5. Your child's **individual needs** have been met.	❏	❏	❏	❏
6. I (Tom) have been **friendly and supportive.**	❏	❏	❏	❏
7. **Parent-teacher conferences and written reports** have been helpful.	❏	❏	❏	❏

8. **Portfolio Night was** _____

9. **I am surprised that** _____

   I am happiest about _____

   I am interested in _____

   I am disappointed that _____

   I am wondering how _____

10. What should NCS **start** doing?

    What should NCS **stop** doing?

    What should NCS **continue** doing?

11. **Other thoughts, questions, observations?** (Use and attach additional pages, if needed.)

D

Sample Letters to Parents

April 30, 2004

Dear Parents,

Last week's early dismissal and inservice day were quite productive. The three sessions (Thursday afternoon, Friday morning, and Friday afternoon) were used to address the three essential components of New City School: *academics, ambience,* and *diversity.*

On Thursday afternoon, we focused on multiple intelligences (MI). Each grade-level team shared one of its MI activities. (Although this activity could fall under *academics* or, for that matter, *diversity,* I count it as *ambience* because MI helps create the environment in which kids learn.) The 1st grade team, for example, shared a list of the MI centers at which students work during their language time. (Each day, children spend some of their language time in guided reading groups with a teacher and the rest of their time among MI centers.) Recent weekly choices for MI centers included a musical center where students read words to the beat of a metronome, a naturalist center where they compared and contrasted a pansy and a marigold, and an intrapersonal center where they wrote about their vegetable likes and dislikes. Each grade (and our specialists) shared ways that MI can be used to enable more students to learn and to enable students to learn more. Using MI creates a learning environment in which more students will be successful because they have done some of their learning in areas of strength and interest.

On Friday morning, our faculty focused on *diversity.* We began with an exercise in which we sorted ourselves by our backgrounds and a range of variables (such as our religion, where we grew up, where we live now, our age, our socioeconomic status growing up and today, and so on). We must have classified and reclassified ourselves more than a dozen times. We then looked at the impact that our history has on us as teachers. How has growing up this way or that way affected our teaching, and how does being an X or a Y continue to affect us today?

On Friday afternoon, we worked on *academics,* aligning our logical-mathematical curriculum with our progress report. The teachers also worked with adjacent grades to develop grade-level benchmarks and to make sure that the math curriculum flows seamlessly from grade to grade.

These sessions cause me to be optimistic about the future. As good as this school year has been, next year will be even better!

Sincerely,

Thomas R. Hoerr, PhD
Head of School
trhoerr@newcityschool.org

May 13, 2004

Dear Parents,

Wondering about the merit of making a request for next year's teacher? First, all our classrooms are heterogeneously balanced. In other words, we try to make each of the rooms in a given grade comparable in terms of students' skills, "teacher time" needs, gender, and race. That is a bit like trying to draw a perfect circle freehand; we never quite get there, but that doesn't mean that we don't try. *In terms of requesting teachers, as in the past, we will accept your requests but do not encourage them.* (If you do wish to share your thoughts, they should be less about personnel and more in terms of your child's strengths, needs, and interests as a learner and a friend.)

That said, you will need to trust that our judgment about student placement is good, even if it doesn't agree with your preference! Yes, you may have heard that Al Einstein is the best teacher in the world, and you just know that your child, Bruno, will shine in his class. However, we may see Bruno differently. Despite the fact that you want him to have Al's hugs, we may think Bruno will prosper under a bit tighter regime. Or maybe you want that crack-the-whip teacher, and we think Bruno needs more of a nurturer. The "we," of course, isn't just me; the "we" represents all our faculty and all our years of experience in placing kids. We're happy to hear your three cents, but know that it will only be one factor in our deciding where to place students.

Finally, all our teachers are very, very strong or else they wouldn't still be teaching here. We have a performance pay plan at New City School. Although all our teachers are caring and work hard, that is not enough. In order to remain here, teachers must care and work hard, but they must also be good teachers and learners. That is true for each and every one of our faculty members. The expectations are quite high, but that is the way that it should be.

Sincerely,

Thomas R. Hoerr, PhD
Head of School
trhoerr@newcityschool.org

References

Angelou, M. (1970). *I know why the caged bird sings.* New York: Random House.

Armas, G. (2004, March 18). Prediction for 2050: Minorities approach half of population. *St. Louis Post-Dispatch*, pp. 1–2.

Bandura, A. (1997). *Self-efficacy: The exercise of control.* New York: W. H. Freeman.

Barth, R. (1980). *Run school run.* Cambridge, MA: Harvard University Press.

Barth, R. (1990). *Improving schools from within: Teachers, parents, and principals can make the difference.* San Francisco: Jossey-Bass.

Barth, R. (Speaker). (2002). *Learning by heart* [Cassette Recording]. Alexandria, VA: Association for Supervision and Curriculum Development.

Barth, R. (2004). *Learning by heart.* San Francisco: Jossey-Bass.

Beals, M. (1994). *Warriors don't cry.* New York: Pocket Books.

Bolman, L., & Deal, T. (1997). *Reframing organizations: Artistry, choice, and leadership.* San Francisco: Jossey-Bass.

Brooks, J., & Brooks, M. (1999). *In search of understanding: The case for constructivist classrooms.* Alexandria, VA: Association for Supervision and Curriculum Development.

Brooks, R. (2002). The merger of flesh and machines. In J. Brockman (Ed.), *The next fifty years* (pp. 183–193). New York: Vintage Books.

Callahan, R. (1962). *Education and the cult of efficiency: A study of the social forces that have shaped the administration of public schools.* Chicago: University of Chicago Press.

Dauten, D. (2003, December 23). The corporate curmudgeon. *St. Louis Post-Dispatch*.

Deal, T., & Peterson, K. (2003). *Shaping school culture: The heart of leadership.* San Francisco: Jossey-Bass.

Diamond, J. (1999). *Guns, germs, and steel: The fates of human societies.* New York: W. W. Norton.

Drucker, P. (1992). *Managing the nonprofit organization: Practices and principles.* New York: HarperCollins.

Drucker, P. (1999). *Management challenges for the 21st century.* New York: Harper-Collins.

Early, G. (1994). *Daughters.* Reading, MA: Addison Wesley.

Faculty of the New City School. (1994). *Celebrating multiple intelligences: Teaching for success.* St. Louis, MO: The New City School.

Faculty of the New City School. (1996). *Succeeding with multiple intelligences: Teaching through the personal intelligences.* St. Louis, MO: The New City School.

Florida, R. (2002). *The rise of the creative class: And how it's transforming work, leisure, community, and everyday life.* New York: BasicBooks.

French, J., & Raven, B. (1959). The bases of social power. In D. Cartwright (Ed.), *Studies in social power* (pp. 150–165). Ann Arbor, MI: Institute for Social Research.

Gardner, H. (1983). *Frames of mind: The theory of multiple intelligences.* New York: BasicBooks.

Gardner, H. (1991). *The unschooled mind: How children think and how schools should teach.* New York: BasicBooks.

Goleman, D. (1995). *Emotional intelligence.* New York: Bantam Books.

Gurian, M. (2001). *Boys and girls learn differently: A guide for teachers and parents.* San Francisco: Jossey-Bass.

Halberstam, D. (2004, September). The greatness that cannot be taught. *Fast Company, 86,* 62.

Hassel, B., & Hassel, E. (2004, September 15). Parents take choice driver's seat, but few have a map. *Education Week, 24*(3), 34–36.

Hoerr, T. (2000). *Becoming a multiple intelligences school.* Alexandria, VA: Association for Supervision and Curriculum Development.

Hoerr, T. (2004, September). The principal connection: New year, new goals. *Educational Leadership, 62*(1), 86–87.

Internet World Stats. (2005). *Internet usage statistics—the big picture: World Internet users and population stats.* Retrieved May 10, 2005, from http://www.internetworldstats.com/stats.htm

Kurzweil, R. (1999). *The age of spiritual machines: When computers exceed human intelligence.* New York: Viking Press.

Kurzweil, R. (2002). The evolution of mind. In J. W. Richards (Ed.), *Are we spiritual machines? Ray Kurzweil vs. the critics of strong A.I.* (pp. 12–55). Seattle, WA: Discovery Institute Press.

Levine, M. (2003). *A mind at a time.* New York: Simon & Schuster.

Machiavelli, N. (1998). *The prince.* Cambridge, England: Cambridge University Press.

Marzano, R., Norford, J., Paynter, D., Pickering, D., & Gaddy, B. (2001). *A handbook for classroom instruction that works.* Alexandria, VA: Association for Supervision and Curriculum Development.

Mintzberg, H. (1998, November–December). Covert leadership: Notes on managing professionals. *Harvard Business Review, 76*(6), 140–147.

Murphy, S. (2002). Leader self-regulation: The role of self-efficacy and multiple intelligences. In R. Riggio, S. Murphy, & F. Pirozzolo (Eds.), *Multiple intelligences and leadership* (pp. 163–186). Mahwah, NJ: Lawrence Erlbaum Associates.

Nohria, N., Joyce, W., & Robinson, B. (2003, July). What really works. *Harvard Business Review, 81*(7), 42–52.

O'Toole, J. (1995). *Leading change: Overcoming the ideology of comfort and the tyranny of custom.* San Francisco: Jossey-Bass.

Oppenheimer, T. (2003). *The flickering mind: The false promise of technology in the classroom, and how learning can be saved.* New York: Random House.

Ouchi, W. (2003). *Making schools work: A revolutionary plan to get your children the education they need.* New York: Simon & Schuster.

Paley, V. (1979). *White teacher.* Cambridge, MA: Harvard University Press.

Peters, T., & Waterman, R. (1982). *In search of excellence: Lessons from America's best-run companies.* New York: Harper & Row.

Read, P. (2005, February 10). University of Phoenix puts technology at learning's forefront. [Electronic version]. *Spokane Journal of Business.*

Rowling, J. K. (2000). *Harry Potter and the goblet of fire.* New York: Scholastic Press.

Salomon, G. (Ed.). (1993). *Distributed cognition: Psychological and educational considerations.* Cambridge, England: Cambridge University Press.

Senge, P. (1990). *The fifth discipline: The art and practice of the learning organization.* New York: Doubleday/Currency.

Smith, A. (1998). *The no. 1 ladies' detective agency.* New York: Anchor Books.

Tatum, B. (1997). *Why are all the black kids sitting together in the cafeteria?* New York: BasicBooks.

Tomlinson, C. A. (2001). *How to differentiate instruction in mixed-ability classrooms* (2nd ed.). Alexandria, VA: Association for Supervision and Curriculum Development.

Tucker, P., & Stronge, J. (2005). *Linking teacher evaluation and student learning.* Alexandria, VA: Association for Supervision and Curriculum Development.

Wagner, T. (2001, January). Leadership for learning. *Phi Delta Kappan, 82*(5), 378–383.

Wetlaufer, S. (2000, July). Who wants to manage a millionaire? *Harvard Business Review, 78*(4).

Resources

In addition to the References, the following resources were help-ful to me in thinking about the issues addressed in this book.

Brown, E. (2004, December 12). Can for-profit schools pass an ethics test? *New York Times*, p. B5.

Collins, J. (2001). *Good to great: Why some companies make the leap—and others don't*. New York: HarperBusiness.

Evans, R. (1996). *The human side of school change: Reform, resistance, and the real-life problems of innovation*. San Francisco: Jossey-Bass.

Fullan, M. (2001). *Leading in a culture of change*. San Francisco: Jossey-Bass.

Gardner, H. (1996). *Leading minds: An anatomy of leadership*. New York: Harper-Collins.

Gittell, J. (2003). *The Southwest Airlines way: Using the power of relationships to achieve high performance*. New York: McGraw-Hill.

Gladwell, M. (2000). *The Tipping Point*. Boston: Little & Brown.

Goodwin, B. (2002). In the shadow of culture. In J. Brockman (Ed.), *The next fifty years* (pp. 41–51). New York: Vintage Books.

Hirsch, E. D. (1988). *Cultural literacy: What every American needs to know*. New York: Vintage Books.

Inclusion Network. (n.d.). Retrieved May 10, 2005, from www.inclusion.org

Lambert, L., Walker, D., Zimmerman, D., Cooper, J., Lambert, M., Gardner, M., & Slack, P. (1995). *The constructivist leader*. New York: Teachers College Press.

Micklethwait, J., & Wooldridge, A. (1996). *The witch doctors: Making sense of the man-agement gurus*. London: Random House.

Putnam, R. (2000). *Bowling alone: The collapse and revival of American community*. New York: Simon & Schuster.

Sarason, S. (1999). *Teaching as a performing art*. New York: Teachers College Press.

Stewart, T. (1997). *Intellectual capital: The new wealth of organizations*. New York: Doubleday/Currency.

Surowiecki, J. (2004). *The wisdom of crowds: Why the many are smarter than the few and how collective wisdom shapes business, economies, societies, and nations*. New York: Doubleday.

Index

Page numbers followed by *f* indicate figures.

About the Author

Photo by Kimberley Keefe

Thomas R. Hoerr has been the head of New City School in St. Louis, Missouri, since 1981. Prior to that he was a principal in the School District of University City, Missouri, and a teacher in two other school districts. Tom founded, directed, and taught in the Washington University Nonprofit Management Program. He has taught graduate classes in leadership and given presentations at many conferences.

Understanding the power of Edward Albee's words, "I write to find out what I am thinking," Tom has written *Becoming a Multiple Intelligences School* (2000) and more than 50 articles. His writing often centers on multiple intelligences implementation, school leadership, and faculty collegiality. Tom holds a doctorate in educational policymaking and program development from Washington University, a master's degree from the University of Missouri–St. Louis, and a bachelor's degree from Harris Teachers College. He can be reached at New City School, 5209 Waterman Avenue, St. Louis, MO 63108 or at trhoerr@newcityschool.org.

Related ASCD Resources: School Leadership

At the time of publication, the following ASCD resources were available; for the most up-to-date information about ASCD resources, go to www.ascd.org. ASCD stock numbers are noted in parentheses.

Audio
Balanced Leadership: What Research Shows About Leadership and Student Achievement by Tim Waters, Robert J. Marzano, and Brian McNulty (2 Audiotapes #204169; 2 CDs #504303)
Changing Schools Through Changing Leadership by Kathy O'Neill (2 Audiotapes #204253; 2 CDs #504387)
Collegiality: The Most Powerful Tool for School Improvement by Thomas R. Hoerr (Audiotape #204091; CD #504125)
Powerful Stories to Help New Principals Build Vibrant Learning Communities by Harvey Alvy and Pam Robbins (Audiotape #204206; CD #504340)

Networks
Visit the ASCD Web site (www.ascd.org) and click on About ASCD. Go to the section on Networks for information about professional educators who have formed groups around topics such as "Multiple Intelligences," "Performance Assessment for Leadership," and "Women's Leadership Issues." Look in the Network Directory for current facilitators' addresses and phone numbers.

Online Courses
Visit the ASCD Web site (www.ascd.org) for the following professional development opportunities:
Contemporary School Leadership by Vera Blake (#PD04OC38)
Effective Leadership by Frank Betts (#PD98OC04)

Print Products
Becoming a Multiple Intelligences School by Thomas R. Hoerr (#100006)
Educational Leadership, April 2004: Leading in Tough Times (Entire Issue #104029)
Finding Your Leadership Style: A Guide for Educators by Jeffrey Glanz (#102115)
Guide for Instructional Leaders, Guide 1: An ASCD Action Tool by Roland Barth, Bobb Darnell, Laura Lipton, and Bruce Wellman (#702110)
Leadership Capacity for Lasting School Improvement by Linda Lambert (#102283)
Leadership for Learning: How to Help Teachers Succeed by Carl D. Glickman (#101031)
Lessons from Exceptional School Leaders by Mark Goldberg (#101229)
On Becoming a School Leader: A Person-Centered Challenge by Arthur W. Combs, Ann B. Miser, and Kathryn S. Whitaker (#199024)

Video
Becoming a Multiple Intelligences School: A Books-in-Action Video with Thomas R. Hoerr (Videotape #400213; 10 Books and 1 Video Package #700218)
The Principal Series Tapes 1–7: *The Evolving Role of the Principal, Creating a Collaborative Learning Community, Survival Tips, Principal as Culture Shaper, Principal as Manager, Principal as Instructional Leader, Principal as Ambassador* with Richard DuFour and Karen Dyer (7 Videotapes and 2 Facilitator's Guides #499242)

For more information, visit us on the World Wide Web (www.ascd.org), send an e-mail message to member@ascd.org, call the ASCD Service Center (1-800-933-ASCD or 703-578-9600, then press 2), send a fax to 703-575-5400, or write to Information Services, ASCD, 1703 N. Beauregard St., Alexandria, VA 22311-1714 USA.